Taming Leviathan

Waging the War of Ideas Around the World

Two week loan
Benthyciad pythefnos

Please return on or before the due date to avoid overdue charges
A wnewch chi ddychwelyd ar neu cyn y dyddiad a nodir ar eich llyfr os gwelwch yn dda, er mwyn osgoi taliadau

Taming Leviathan

Waging the War of Ideas Around the World

EDITED BY COLLEEN DYBLE

The Institute of Economic Affairs

First published in Great Britain in 2008 by
The Institute of Economic Affairs
2 Lord North Street
Westminster
London SW1P 3LB
in association with Profile Books Ltd

The mission of the Institute of Economic Affairs is to improve public understanding of the fundamental institutions of a free society, by analysing and expounding the role of markets in solving economic and social problems.

A CIP catalogue record for this book is available from the British Library.

ISBN 978 0 255 36607 6

Many IEA publications are translated into languages other than English or are reprinted. Permission to translate or to reprint should be sought from the Director General at the address above.

Typeset in Stone by MacGuru Ltd
info@macguru.org.uk

Printed and bound in Great Britain by Hobbs the Printers

CONTENTS

5 The battle of ideas in Chile: the case of Libertad y Desarrollo

6 University Francisco Marroquín: a model for winning liberty

THE AUTHORS

Daniel Doron

Daniel Doron is the Director and Founder of the Israel Centre for Social and Economic Progress (ICSEP). Doron helped found Israel's Shinui (Change) Party, serves on various economic advisory boards, and appears frequently on Israeli and international TV and radio, as well as in print. Prior to ICSEP, he served in Air Force Intelligence during Israel's 1948 War of Independence and served as Special Consultant to the US Embassy in Tel Aviv. Doron studied sociology and economics at the Hebrew University and was a fellow at the University of Chicago's Committee on Social Thought and a Visiting Scholar at Columbia University. He teaches seminars at several Israeli universities and is a member of the Mont Pèlerin Society.

Colleen Dyble

Colleen Dyble is the Director of Coalition Relations at the Atlas Economic Research Foundation. In this capacity, Dyble facilitates coalitions among domestic and international think tanks and provides them with resources and contacts. She has developed and executed think tank management and economic policy networking conferences throughout Africa, Asia, Europe and North America, and regularly represents Atlas at international events. Dyble was a teaching assistant and guest lecturer at the Fund for American Studies' American Institute on Political and Economic Systems in Prague, Czech Republic, and served on the Advisory Board of the African Growth and Opportunity Act (AGOA) Civil Society Network. She received her bachelor's degree in International Political Economy and Spanish from the University of Puget Sound and her master's degree in International Commerce and Policy from George Mason University.

Giancarlo Ibárgüen S.

Giancarlo Ibárgüen S. is the Executive President of the Universidad Francisco Marroquín in Guatemala, as well as an entrepreneur, educator and financial adviser to various companies. His articles on economics and telecommunications have been widely published throughout the international media and he has contributed to several publications of the Centre for Economic and Social Studies (CEES) in Guatemala. Ibárgüen received his Bachelor of Science in Electrical Engineering from Texas A&M University. He serves on the board of numerous liberty-oriented and private sector organisations and he is a member of the Mont Pèlerin Society and the Philadelphia Society.

Cristián Larroulet

Cristián Larroulet is the Executive Director of Libertad y Desarrollo, a private think tank in Chile, and a founder and current Dean of the economics faculty at the Universidad de

Desarrollo. Larroulet has published numerous books and scholarly articles in the areas of privatisation, public finance, economic regulation and economic and social development and is a regular columnist in the Chilean newspaper *La Tercera*. He is a member of the Mont Pèlerin Society and of the Chilean Academy of Social, Political and Moral Sciences.

Greg Lindsay

Greg Lindsay is the founder and Executive Director of the Centre for Independent Studies in Australia. While studying philosophy at Macquarie University in the early 1970s, Lindsay became interested in the ideas underpinning a free and open society. A maths teacher by training, Lindsay taught for some years at Richmond Boys' High School before founding the Centre in 1976. Mr Lindsay has been active in the international liberal movement and is currently President of the Mont Pèlerin Society.

Elena Leontjeva

Elena Leontjeva is the founder and former President of the Lithuanian Free Market Institute (LFMI) and currently serves on its board of directors. At the Institute, she was actively involved in establishing Lithuania's securities market and stock exchange, implementing banking reform and creating a currency board system. In 1994, Leontjeva became State Councillor on economic reform issues and served in this position in seven consecutive administrations. She later served as the Economic Adviser to President Adamkus. She has published widely in the press and her input has been instrumental in tax, social security and institutional reforms. Leontjeva resigned from the presidency of LFMI in 2001 to dedicate herself to fiction writing.

Leon Louw

Leon Louw is the Executive Director of the Free Market Foundation and the Law Review project in South Africa. Louw is a well-known speaker, the author of many published articles, and the co-author of two books, *South Africa: The Solution* and *Let the People Govern*. He is a member of the Mont Pèlerin Society and has delivered papers and addressed audiences in over thirty countries. Louw has been nominated for the Nobel Peace Prize on a number of occasions.

Alex Magno

Alex R. Magno is the President of the Foundation for Economic Freedom in the Philippines and a Professor of Political Science at the University of the Philippines. He is also the President of Stratdev Inc., a consulting firm, and Director of the government-owned Development Bank of the Philippines, where he oversees finance infrastructure programmes for disadvantaged provinces. Magno writes a thrice-weekly editorial column for the *Philippine Star* and chairs the Centrist Policy Institute, a think tank advising the ruling Lakas party.

Alberto Mingardi

Alberto Mingardi is the General Director of the Istituto Bruno Leoni in Italy, of which he was a founder in 2003. He is also a

Senior Fellow at the Centre for New Europe in Brussels. He has worked at various public policy organisations in the United States, including the Acton Institute, the Atlas Economic Research Foundation and the Heritage Foundation. Mingardi translated Antonio Rosmini's *The Constitution According to Social Justice* into English and edited a few volumes. His articles have been published in numerous international newspapers and journals. Mingardi specialises in political philosophy and holds a degree in Political Science from the University of Pavia.

Parth Shah

Dr Parth J. Shah is President of the Centre for Civil Society in India. His work centres on the themes of economic freedom, choice and competition in education, and property rights. He conceptualises and organises classical liberal educational programmes for young people, appears frequently in print media, and speaks at numerous national and international conferences. Shah is on the editorial board of *EducationWorld*, *Vishleshan* and *Khoj*, and is an informal adviser to many non-profit organisations. He has edited numerous books and is the youngest Indian member of the Mont Pèlerin Society.

Margaret Tse

Margaret Tse is the CEO of Instituto Liberdade, the Director of HoldTse Investments and Equities Inc. and a public policy researcher. She was born in Brazil, but her family came from Shanghai (China) in 1948. She holds a bachelor's degree in Business and Public Administration from the University of Rio

Grande do Sul (Brazil) and a doctorate in Business Administration from the Asia Pacific International University (Canada), and has taught at the Pontifical Catholic University of Rio Grande do Sul. She received the Libertas Award in 2006 and a Distinguished Women Award in 2007.

Masaru Uchiyama

Masaru Uchiyama is the Founder and President of the Japanese for Tax Reform in Japan. He is a former executive manager of a medium-sized company in Japan and is featured in the Heritage Foundation's *Policy Experts* guide. In 2007, the Japanese for Tax Reform became the first Japanese organisation to receive a Templeton Freedom Award from the Atlas Economic Research Foundation.

Bridgett Wagner

As Director of the Coalition Relations Department at the Heritage Foundation, Bridgett Wagner advises think tanks on ways to build support for their policy prescriptions and builds support for the Heritage research agenda 'beyond the Washington Beltway'. She edits Heritage's biennial *Policy Experts* directory and the online PolicyExperts.org, and oversees the InsiderOnline.org and its accompanying quarterly, *The Insider: Conservative Solutions for Advancing Liberty*. Wagner is a trustee of the State Policy Network and the International Policy Network. She also serves on the Advisory Board of the Council on Public Policy (Germany), the Executive Advisory Board of the Adriatic Institute for Public Policy (Croatia), and is a member of the Mont Pèlerin Society.

Michael Walker

Michael Walker, PhD, LLD, is a Senior Fellow at the Fraser Institute in Canada, of which he was Executive Director for 30 years, in which capacity he wrote articles, books, radio programmes and more than 700 opinion-editorials. Before that he worked at the Bank of Canada and the Federal Department of Finance. He is a director of public and private equity firms, the owner of the Prado Verde Group and a Director of the Friedman Foundation for Educational Choice.

Atilla Yayla

Atilla Yayla is the co-founder and President of the Association for Liberal Thinking in Turkey. He is a Professor of Political Philosophy and Political Economy at Gazi University in Ankara and regularly writes op-eds in the Turkish national daily newspapers. Yayla is the author of many articles and books in Turkish, including *Liberalism*; *Introduction to Political Theory*; and *Dictionary of Political Thought*, and is the editor of *Islam, Civil Society and Market Economy* in English. He is a member of the Mont Pèlerin Society.

FOREWORD

In 2001, the Institute of Economic Affairs (IEA) published an Occasional Paper that collected the writings and speeches of its Director General and Ralph Harris Fellow, John Blundell. It outlined the history and operations of that venerable institution and described the impact the IEA had on the intellectual and political climate in the UK. *Waging the War of Ideas* was a slim volume that packed a powerful message: ideas have consequences; individuals who argue from principle and with persistence can change the policy debates and, ultimately, the history of their country; and, as Ed Feulner, President of the Heritage Foundation, often remarks, there are no permanent victories or defeats in this war – the battle must be fought and refought again with each new government and new generation.

Waging the War of Ideas provided a battlefield manual for those on the intellectual front lines. Copies were highlighted, quoted and handed out to colleagues around the world. And by the time the third (and expanded) edition was released in 2007, Internet downloads and email exchanges were the preferred means of sharing timely passages in the heat of the battle. The most recent exchange I witnessed occurred on the 'AfricaClub' e-list earlier this month (March 2008). The recent election in Kenya and subsequent violence had made this a very active discussion forum. Contributors learned the latest news and the status of political negotiations from the Kenyan leaders on the list. They debated the best ways to establish the rule of law, expand freedom and promote prosperity. Op-eds, quotes and commentary were provided daily, and along the way a reference was made and a link provided to *Waging the War of Ideas*. An endorsement from Ghana confirmed the power and reach of this little volume.

This new volume, *Taming Leviathan: Waging the War of Ideas around the World*, builds on the earlier work and shares the experiences of thirteen institute leaders from different countries. Starting with the successful example of Australia's Centre for Independent Study, Greg Lindsay shares a personal and institutional history that will be familiar to many policy entrepreneurs. Brazil's Margaret Tse provides background on the development of her country as well as the spread of ideas through translations and the work of the Instituto Liberdade. Michael Walker of the Fraser Institute emphasises the importance of fact-based analysis in a think tank's work. 'If it matters, measure it' is their mantra, and they have produced a line of products that has mobilised citizens' concerns about their own wallets and the direct impact of policies on their family circumstances.

The Chilean case study, outlined by Cristián Larroulet of Libertad y Desarrollo, provides a wonderful example of how ideas move from the academy to the popularisers to the politicians. And their impact is confirmed each year with Chile's ranking in the indexes that measure economic freedom. Giancarlo Ibárgüen of Guatemala tells the story of a group of 'rebellious improvisers' and the impressive university they founded. By focusing on 'essential themes that transcend contemporary issues' they have educated an intellectual elite and influenced policy decisions in that country.

Parth Shah of the Centre for Civil Society took his American experience and returned to India to awaken a 'slumbering elephant'. His strategy, which was arrived at after developing a matrix of five think tank models, focuses on influencing civil society – the domain of voluntary action – through research, advocacy campaigns, pilot projects and policymaking. It is important to show what works because, as Shah notes, 'Unless people see civil society alternatives working, they will be very reluctant to let the state withdraw.'

Israel's Daniel Doron first argued for political reforms in his country in the 1970s. His group's struggle to raise funds and garner support for their fledgling 'Movement for Change' led him to understand the link between political and economic freedom. Potential supporters were reluctant to alienate 'a government upon whom they were dependent in so many ways (subsidies, special tax concessions, permits, land zoning, etc.)'. He saw that economic growth and liberalisation were the key to solving so many of his country's problems, and the Israel Centre for Social and Economic Progress set out to provide 'the know-how needed to fashion, implement and support pro-market structural reforms and the intellectual ammunition to overcome resistance to them'.

Alberto Mingardi notes that Italy has not been lacking 'intellectual ammunitions against statism', but it did lack the intermediaries that have proven necessary to 'bridge the gap between theory and policy proposals'. As Mingardi notes, the challenge for any think tank or policy entrepreneur is to get the intellectual movement actively integrated in the real world. From the beginning the Istituto Bruno Leoni engaged in the public policy debates against the more established and better-armed trade unions and business associations. While not 'watering down' the consistency of their ideas, they remained open to opportunities to advance incremental reforms. And in the process their entrepreneurial style has attracted a growing audience of politicians, journalists and young intellectuals and launched the beginning of a new debate in Italy.

Masaru Uchiyama and his Japanese for Tax Reform (JTR) have helped to educate the public on the tax burden in that country and to foster collaboration among the think tanks, grassroots coalitions and educational institutions. As one of the few non-profit organisations in Japan that does not receive government funds, JTR has been able to maintain its independence from the political parties and more effectively preach the benefits of small government.

Five young scholars and their professor set out to build a new order in the newly liberated Lithuania. As Elena Leontjeva notes, this new order was to be built on individual liberty and limited government. Even though they were young and in many ways inexperienced, the reform proposals of the Lithuania Free Market Institute competed on an equal footing with proposals coming out of government ministries. And while financing for their operation was difficult to come by, the most crucial donation was their 'efforts … which were donated for free to the free market cause. This was the key investment that formed the foundation of the institute'. Of course, they were not able to address all the pressing problems of the day, but they prudently chose the most central ones which would result in a chain reaction (wise counsel for start-ups in a rapidly changing political or policy environment). In the process they have become an incubator for statesmen and a recruiting ground for government ministers, councillors, central bankers and key advisers.

The Philippines' Alexander Magno describes the challenges of operating in a populist democracy where the loudest protests shape the policy outcomes. Economic literacy is in short supply and powerful lobby groups dominate the debates. The Foundation for Economic Freedom was born to take on these challenges with impeccable research, superior argumentation and a network of high-profile scholars who have effectively utilised the media and formed alliances with outside groups. Magno's own experience in left-wing academic and political circles has made him an effective advocate for free market policies because he sees them as superior in moving society towards the vision of freedom, prosperity and democracy.

Leon Louw of South Africa returns to analogies of the battlefield in his analysis of think tank styles: aerial bombardment (influencing the climate of opinion over time) versus trench warfare (engaging in 'practical' and 'pragmatic' activities designed to influence a more imminent proposed reform). Louw outlines the relative merits of each style for mature democracies and developing countries. He notes that previously effective strategies and tactics are not likely to be effective when the battle lines are not so starkly drawn as during the cold war, when capitalism/liberalism fought communism/socialism. The differences between political parties may be blurred and the enemies of liberty today portray themselves as benign or concerned. Louw says that in this new environment his Free Market Foundation has converted its message from 'being overtly ideological to being empirical', and in the process he believes they have enhanced their relevance.

Finally, Atilla Yayla outlines the long and lonely journey of two academics responsible for building a freedom movement in Turkey. They read day and night to shape their views and eventually were able to travel and meet fellow defenders of the free market economy. They were inspired to launch an intellectual movement, and working with students and volunteers they set up the Association for Liberal Thinking (ALT), which now publishes translations and scholarly journals, hosts seminars and congresses, and provides an academic advisory service. Today, the ALT is the most important intellectual movement in Turkey and, Yayla confidently proclaims, 'one day, those individuals who were brought up with the ideas that ALT defends will run Turkey'. Theirs is a patient strategy well suited to this country in transition.

In reviewing each case study one is struck by several recurring themes: the importance of books and the spread of ideas; the international nature of the network that sustains and energises these leaders; how many started out on the intellectual left, but saw that it was the free market that best served the individual; and always, the *never-ending* nature of this work.

As Leon Louw notes in his chapter, 'it seems increasingly clear that the price of freedom is indeed eternal vigilance, that there is no end of ideological history, and that power reasserts itself against liberty eternally, changing substantially in form, but never in substance'. The freedom movement has grown substantially since the first of these institutes was formed. Their books, journals and conferences have multiplied and gone online, but the real power still resides in the ideas argued persuasively by individuals who fight on the front lines in the war of ideas.

BRIDGETT WAGNER
Director of Coalition Relations at the Heritage Foundation
March 2008

The views expressed in this monograph are, as in all IEA publications, those of the author and not those of the Institute (which has no corporate view), its managing trustees, Academic Advisory Council members or senior staff.

1 INTRODUCTION
Colleen Dyble, Atlas Economic Research Foundation

Half a century ago, no one could have foreseen that a condensed version of Friedrich Hayek's *The Road to Serfdom* by the *Reader's Digest* would inspire Antony Fisher, a World War II Royal Air Force fighter pilot, chicken farmer and self-made millionaire, to change the course of history. Fisher was concerned about encroaching socialism and central planning, in his native Britain as well as overseas, so in 1945 he went to meet Hayek at the London School of Economics, where the great economist was a faculty member. This encounter was a turning point for both Fisher and the history of ideas.

Encouraged by Hayek to counter the then dominant ideological trend towards socialism by engaging intellectuals through reasoned arguments rather than politics, Fisher became a major catalyst behind the global rise of classical liberal and libertarian think tanks. In 1955, he founded the Institute of Economic Affairs (IEA), Britain's original free market think tank. Directed by Ralph Harris, the IEA laid the intellectual framework for what later became the Thatcher Revolution. It would also become a model for think tank leaders around the world who shared Fisher's concern about the emergence of central planning in their own countries.

Building upon IEA Director General John Blundell's *Waging the War of Ideas*, which documents the success of the IEA in fighting central planning in Britain in the 1960s and 1970s, *Taming Leviathan: Waging the War of Ideas around the World* explores the climate of intellectual debate in thirteen different countries. The book looks at how classical liberal ideas, ignited and transmitted through the work of think tanks, have transformed intellectual debate and led to significant victories in the battle for economic freedom and prosperity.

Intellectual entrepreneurs have been essential to those victories. Just as a dynamic economy needs entrepreneurs to develop new ideas and bring innovations to the market, intellectual entrepreneurs strive to bring new ideas to the public policy debate.

The intellectual entrepreneurs featured in this book bridge the gap between the academic and policymaking communities – by promoting public policies that respect private property and the rule of law, encourage entrepreneurship and competition, support independent judiciaries, define boundaries for the role of the state and promote liberty and freedom of choice for all citizens. They hail from around the world – Australia, Brazil, Canada, Chile, Guatemala, India, Israel, Italy, Japan, Lithuania, Philippines, South Africa and Turkey. It is my hope that their stories will encourage you to wage the war of ideas in your own country.

The IEA think tank model, inspired by Hayek and executed by Fisher, has been replicated in nearly a hundred countries around the world in response to the rising tide of socialism and expanding government intervention and control. The intellectual entrepreneurs profiled in this volume certainly applied it in their own countries – where it was desperately needed.

It is easy to forget how bad the situation looked in the 1970s. Socialism infiltrated universities in Latin America, particularly in Guatemala, which became a breeding ground for Marxism. Social and political discontent was on the rise in Australia, Canada and South Africa, as governments failed to control inflation and increased their intervention in the economy through protectionism and wage and price controls. Likewise, in Brazil during the mid-1980s, the growth of 'positivism' (stemming from Portuguese colonisation) encouraged 'socially responsible authoritarianism' and led to higher taxes, extensive red tape, land invasions, corruption and an unreliable judicial system. The nationalisation of the oil industry brought government regulation of oil prices in the Philippines in the mid-1990s. High tax burdens on Japanese citizens and growing government corruption in Italy fuelled government expansion in those countries.

A keen awareness of the challenges to liberty and a solid fluency in classical liberal thought gave the authors the intellectual ammunition they needed to do battle against socialism in their own countries. All of these authors have different stories to tell about what prompted them to utilise think tanks as their main weapon.

An excitement about libertarian ideas – and the need to inject them into public debate – spurred young intellectuals in Brazil, Italy, Japan, the Philippines and Turkey to found think tanks. Brazil's Instituto Liberdade, of which Margaret Tse (Chapter 3) is CEO, was founded to fill a gap in intellectual debates and persuade Brazilian citizens of the advantages of a classical liberal order. An internship at the Heritage Foundation in Washington, DC, tutelage under Lord Harris and the work of other think tanks in Europe encouraged Alberto Mingardi (Chapter 9) to start the Istituto Bruno Leoni in Italy. Masaru Uchiyama (Chapter 10) was inspired by the work of Grover Norquist at Americans for Tax Reform to start a similar institute, Japanese for Tax Reform. Alex

Magno (Chapter 12), President of the Foundation for Economic Freedom in the Philippines, studied Marxist thought as a young academic before being introduced to libertarian ideas. Similarly, Atilla Yayla (Chapter 14) was a socialist until months of personal study and debates with colleagues led him to discover libertarianism and later start the Association for Liberal Thinking in his native Turkey.

Frustration with socialist government policies and teaching at universities ignited the spark for think tank developments in Australia, Canada, Lithuania, Guatemala, India and Israel. Greg Lindsay (Chapter 2), founder of the Centre for Independent Studies in Australia, started his institute in a two-room backyard shed in 1976 to counter public support for the concept that government was the solution to society's problems. Likewise, the Fraser Institute was founded by Michael Walker (Chapter 4), along with Sally Pipes, John Raybould and Csaba Hajdu, during a time when Canadians believed that government should be the principal source of growth and development in the economy. Elena Leontjeva (Chapter 11), a former president and one of six founders of the Lithuanian Free Market Institute, discovered the power of free market ideas while growing up under a regime that restricted all market activity. Giancarlo Ibárgüen S. in Guatemala (Chapter 6), Parth Shah in India (Chapter 7) and Daniel Doron in Israel (Chapter 8) were inspired to action because of their shared concern about the encroaching socialism they saw in academia and the need to cultivate the next generation of classical liberal thinkers.

Timing has also been significant in the founding of think tanks. Pivotal political and economic transitions in Chile and South Africa created opportunities for think tanks to develop new policy ideas and provide direction to their countries' leaders. Libertad y Desarrollo, directed by Cristián Larroulet (Chapter 5), was founded in 1990 to facilitate Chile's transition to a full market economy. Leon Louw (Chapter 13), Executive Director of the Free Market Foundation since 1978, has had a significant impact on policymaking in South Africa during and after apartheid.

Through research, advocacy and education, these think tank leaders have successfully introduced classical liberal ideas into critical public debates, directly influencing public policy outcomes and legislation. The policy successes of these think tanks include minimising barriers to business creation and market entry, creating stable financial structures, promoting free and open trade, reducing wasteful government spending and unnecessary taxes, and providing increased choice in education. A selection of their achievements is listed below:

- Beginning with a book grant from the Atlas Economic Research Foundation in 1995, the Association for Liberal Thinking published a Turkish translation of Hayek's *The Road to Serfdom*. It has gone on to publish almost two hundred more books, making it a serious player on Turkey's intellectual scene.
- In Italy, where classical liberal ideas were previously rarely aired in public discussion, Istituto Bruno Leoni has helped inject those ideas into public debate.
- Brazil's Instituto Liberdade has helped promote free market solutions to issues such as intellectual property, healthcare, trade, climate change and sustainable development.
- The Fraser Institute has made the concept of economic freedom more tangible to journalists, politicians and the

general public through its annual Economic Freedom of the World index.

- The academic community centred around Universidad Francisco Marroquín participated in Guatemala's constitutional reform of 1993, which prohibits the central bank from lending to the Guatemalan government, and in 1996 influenced Guatemala's congress to pass the most liberal telecommunications law in the world.
- The Israel Centre for Social and Economic Progress has successfully promoted reforms in financial markets and laid the groundwork for anti-inflationary policies in the mid-1980s.
- The Lithuanian Free Market Institute developed the legal framework for the first Lithuanian commodities market and was active in the 1993 opening of the first stock exchange in the former Soviet Union.
- The Centre for Independent Studies was instrumental in convincing Australia's Labor government in the 1980s to reduce regulation and adopt free trade policies.
- Libertad y Desarrollo prevented Chile from reversing progress in free market reforms, while its Executive Director, Cristián Larroulet, has helped design and implement reforms for 27 years in areas such as privatisation, competition and trade liberalisation.
- The Foundation for Economic Freedom was instrumental in opening up the Philippines' telecoms monopoly and supported a comprehensive tax reform package.
- Members of the Free Market Foundation in South Africa helped design national economic policies both before and after the end of apartheid, ensuring they were more pro-freedom.

- Japanese for Tax Reform pioneered the Taxpayers Protection Pledge, which called on Japanese lawmakers to pledge to oppose any new tax increases.
- The Centre for Civil Society has worked to introduce education choice into India through the distribution of thousands of vouchers for primary school children.

Taming Leviathan: Waging the War of Ideas around the World shows that thanks to the engagement of intellectual entrepreneurs in public debates classical liberal ideas are taking hold and having a positive impact in the public policy arena.

On a personal note, my first exposure to a society that severely restricted individual freedom came while I was learning about Francisco Franco in Granada, Spain. Little did I realise that three years later I would be working on a daily basis to diffuse Fisher's think tank model to help people around the world make their countries more free and prosperous.

I am thankful for the opportunity to work with the Atlas Economic Research Foundation. I hope that the lessons in this book from the intellectual entrepreneurs with whom I have had the pleasure to work over the past seven years prove that change is possible when we join the intellectual battles in our own countries to advance freedom. Contemporary threats to liberty are less distinguishable, widespread or overt than Marxism. As champions of classical liberal ideals, we must be expeditious and strategic about developing principled strategies and cultivating the next generation of leaders who will continue and develop the transformative work of our think tanks around the world.

2 A LITTLE BIT OF (INTELLECTUAL) ENTREPRENEURSHIP GOES A LONG WAY
Greg Lindsay, Centre for Independent Studies (Australia)

Australia has been a peaceful and prosperous nation almost since European settlement in 1788. It is one of the world's most stable democracies. For much of the twentieth century what has come to be known as the Australian Settlement drove government and policy. After World War II, the protectionism, labour market regulation, state paternalism and White Australia policy that were key components of the Australian Settlement vision were increasingly seen as ideas from another era. By the 1960s, when I was a teenager, the sense of anachronism was pervasive.

Looking at my early life, it would have been hard to guess that I would end up starting a major think tank. My background was solidly middle class, though by no means especially prosperous – my father died when I was thirteen. My life consisted of family (I was the eldest of three), school, Scouts, and part-time jobs in place of pocket money. I was more interested in bushwalking and skiing than ideas, and my first foray into university studies (in agriculture) was a dismal failure. Since I was on a teacher training scholarship, something had to be done with me, so I was shipped off to teachers' college to study mathematics, an area where I seemed to have some ability. Several faltering years later, I finally qualified.

My university years were politically exciting times for Australia. After 23 years of tired conservative government, the Australian Labor Party, led by Gough Whitlam, won the federal election

in 1972, ousting Prime Minister William McMahon's Liberal/
Country Party coalition. 'It's time' had been Labor's election
slogan, and it truly was its time. But the Australian public were
not quite ready for the government they got, which overspent, saw
inflation rise, and ultimately ended in meltdown in 1975, when the
opposition blocked supply in the Senate. In the ensuing constitutional crisis, the governor-general sacked Whitlam as prime
minister and appointed opposition leader Malcolm Fraser as care-
taker in his place. Fraser won the subsequent election in a land-
slide, but his government proved to be quite a disappointment to
those seeking reform. It was at teachers' college that the world of
ideas started to have an impact on me, but in surprising ways. The
madness of the Whitlam government certainly provoked me into
thinking that their way was a crazy way to run a country. Economically, the signs were less than promising. Inflation getting out of
control was just one indicator.

One of my lecturers at college, the film critic Bill Collins, was a
fan of Ayn Rand: he interspersed education theory with libertarian
philosophy and showings of *The Fountainhead*. 'Now, this is something interesting,' I thought, 'what next?' I started reading, and
entered the world of ideas about classical liberalism and freedom.
Little did I know that world would shape the rest of my life.

But my immediate destiny was still to be a teacher. I had begun
to wonder whether the organisation and provision of education
in Australia were consistent with my developing views about a
free society and the role of education within it. As I suppose any
25-year-old teacher starting out with such ideas does, I decided
that I should start an independent school.

A collection of pamphlets on education and the state began
to fill my shelves. I also started to build my first freedom library,

like so many others, by buying books from the Foundation for Economic Education in New York. Importantly, my reading included F. A. Hayek's 'The intellectuals and socialism', which first appeared in the *University of Chicago Law Review* in 1949, and had been reprinted by the Institute for Humane Studies (IHS). Strategically, this was the most important short article I was to read, because it set out the challenge to which the Centre for Independent Studies (CIS) still rises today: 'we can make the philosophic foundations of a free society once more a living intellectual issue, and its implementation a task which challenges the ingenuity and imagination of our liveliest minds ... if we can regain that belief in the power of ideas which was the mark of liberalism at its best, the battle is not lost'.

In my earlier reading, I had discovered the Center for Independent Education (CIE) in Wichita, Kansas, which was part of the IHS. I began a fruitful correspondence with George Pearson, who ran it. That continued for many years – he remains a friend to this day. In 1975, my first year as a teacher, I travelled to Wichita and visited George and CIE (just a postbox, really), and it was at the Pearson home that I first came across the books of the Institute of Economic Affairs (IEA), about which I had previously known nothing. That lack of knowledge was to change within a short few months. A bigger picture of the world of ideas was emerging.

On that same 1975 trip to the USA, I met Murray Rothbard in New York, where I helped him and his wife stuff envelopes on their living-room floor – good training for running a think tank! Towards the end of the trip, I changed my mind about starting a school. I thought I could do something to remedy the problems that faced Australia, but it would require thinking bigger. I had to face squarely the task Hayek set in 'The intellectuals and socialism'.

The problems were intellectual … it was time for me to do something about them … CIE, IHS and IEA were all centres of intellectual endeavour … 'Forget the school,' I thought, 'this is what I should start!' By the time my plane landed back in Sydney, where I was ready to start my second year of teaching at Richmond High School, the die was cast.

That year, 1976, IEA founder Antony Fisher first visited Australia. He and a group of people were trying to start an IEA-style think tank here. When I found out where he was staying in Sydney, I called him and outlined what I was attempting to do. He wished me luck.

When Fisher returned in December of the same year, I met him at a small meeting he addressed. In October, I had already organised a seminar at Macquarie University with academics John Ray and Lauchlan Chipman as speakers. Chipman, a professor of philosophy, was the first academic I contacted to discuss my plans. It seemed to me that what Fisher was proposing was what I was already doing. I wondered how I could turn that to the Centre's advantage.

I spent the next few years on teaching, further university study in philosophy, and the first steps in building the CIS. In those years, I met some crucial people, including Maurice Newman, who had brought Milton Friedman to Australia in 1975, and Ross Parish, then a professor of economics at Monash University.

Many of the academic connections I had made came together to speak at a conference at Macquarie University in April 1978. The conference drew a decent crowd, including Paddy McGuinness, who was then the economics editor of the *Australian Financial Review*. Two days later, Paddy wrote a famous article about the conference, 'Where Friedman is a pinko', which gave our phone number and address. We were flooded with messages for days. It was a major coup for us.

While still a teacher, I had persuaded my school's principal to let me have some time off and attend the Mont Pèlerin Society (MPS) meeting in Hong Kong in 1978. I became a member of the MPS in 1982, and was eventually elected to the board in 1994. In 2006, I had the honour of being elected the Society's president, which has truly been one of the highlights of my life. I followed as president some great people who have been my heroes – especially Hayek and Friedman. At the start of the 21st century, the MPS endures more strongly than ever as the pre-eminent organisation dedicated to the principles of liberalism. Being a part of it has been of enormous benefit to the development of the CIS.

With the CIS building momentum, something in the other parts of my life had to give, so during 1979 I took leave without pay from my teaching job to try to kick the Centre into life as a full-time enterprise. It was another world for me, and a big risk. Still, my future wife, Jenny, who I had met while she was still at university, was working, and two of the Centre's earliest supporters, Neville Kennard and Ross Graham-Taylor, were also providing some financial support, so we weren't entirely without income. Kennard remains a consistent and major supporter to this day. The group that had been supporting the efforts to start an IEA-style think tank decided that perhaps CIS should be supported after all, but nothing came of it right away.

Eventually, I identified Melbourne businessman Hugh Morgan as a key figure in that IEA effort. I rang him, told him I thought this institute business had stalled, and that it was time to stop the talk. A couple of days later, I flew down to Melbourne to see him, and he decided it was time to move on it. He mustered about

$40,000 per year for five years, and with this small funding base, in 1980 we set up the CIS above Uncle Pete's Toys in St Leonards in Sydney. We stayed there for ten years; that office was where we set out to build our reputation and pursue our mission.

The Centre celebrated its 30th anniversary in 2006 with a sell-out dinner. People who have been members and supporters from day one attended, and they were joined by others, including then prime minister John Howard, cabinet ministers and leaders in politics, business and other fields from across Australia and New Zealand.

Looking back, there have been many highlights. In the early years, we focused almost entirely on economic reform. And by the end of our first decade, in 1986, the impetus for that reform in Australia had been well established. We had a Labor government under Bob Hawke committed to reducing regulation and opening up free trade, and an opposition unlikely to oppose any such moves. It seemed that economic liberalism was the new orthodoxy.

That situation continues to this day, to varying degrees. A century of protectionism in Australia has given way. We are now one of the world's more open economies, with further tariff reductions scheduled within the next few years that will remove much of the remaining protectionism. For 30 years, governments at federal and state levels have privatised enterprises they have controlled for all of living memory. Banks, airlines, pharmaceutical companies, utilities and public transport have all made the transition, and the process continues. If you look at the early work of the CIS, you see numerous examples of published recommendations that became policy over time.

Our work was a key component in the environment for reform, but I can't claim that we were entirely responsible. Nevertheless, there are clear examples where a particular publication led to a policy change. The best known of these is the deregulation of shopping hours in New South Wales soon after we published *Free to Shop* by Geoff Hogbin: the reaction was visible and immediate.

Over the last ten years, we've had a growing interest in international and strategic policy, particularly with regard to China and the Pacific, in Indigenous issues and in health. And social policy has been a focus since the late 1980s. Much of the direction of our most successful work is the result of the contributions of key people. In our early work on economic policy, Ross Parish's contribution was vital. Our currently acknowledged strength in social policy could not have come about without Barry Maley, Peter Saunders and the many younger people who have worked under their guidance. Helen Hughes has steered the way where Indigenous policy and the Pacific are concerned. And if I were to go through our entire list of past and present staff, I could think of some way in which they specifically contributed to the output and life of the CIS, and of the country.

We continue to produce a prodigious amount of material: our back catalogue includes probably over two hundred books and monographs. Our quarterly magazine, *Policy*, currently edited by Andrew Norton, has been going for 23 years; we have a series of almost one hundred Issue Analysis papers and have published thousands of newspaper articles and op-eds. When we have our weekly staff meetings, there is usually an exhaustive list to read out of all our staff's media appearances and mentions.

Seminars, lectures and conferences continue to be a part of CIS activities. This year's annual John Bonython Lecture will be the 25th. Israel Kirzner gave the first of them in 1984 and since then we've had people including James Buchanan, Václav Klaus, Rupert

Murdoch, Mario Vargas Llosa and Ralph Harris on the stage. The Acton Lecture on Religion and Freedom turns ten in 2008, and the Centre's flagship conference, Consilium, which attracts top-level people from the worlds of ideas, business and politics from around the globe, moves into its ninth year. Then there are all kinds of other events, such as our Policymakers series, where political leaders from both sides air their ideas in public, and the annual Big Ideas Forum, which attracts hundreds of people to hear debate on some of the most challenging and interesting ideas of the day.

Sometimes it's suggested to me that the CIS could start or become a university. This doesn't seem likely, but our Liberty and Society programme brings together young people to hear about liberalism and the free society, sometimes for the first time, from liberal intellectuals. Some of those speakers are alumni of the same programme, now academics – so we're having some success in bringing liberalism back into the universities. Liberty and Society harks back to that original impulse I had to start a school, and that mission to involve new people in an intellectual life where economic and personal liberty are key values is still an important driver for the Centre.

These past 30 years and more have been an incredible journey for me, and one that I've been privileged to be able to share with many others. All the institutes I know have stories about how they got to where they are, all different, and this is ours. There will certainly be others that will start on similar paths in the future.

For Australia now, however, I feel it would be more difficult for someone new to do what we have done without substantial start-up support. CIS was the entrepreneurial endeavour of a young man (me) committed to doing something about the threats he and others saw to the free society. It was difficult enough back in 1976! I hope others will try nevertheless, and that they will have the clear vision and thick skin to succeed. Entrepreneurs in any field, as Israel Kirzner reminds us, are always alert to new ways of doing things and correcting what they see as errors. That's pretty much what I set out to do more than thirty years ago. I fully accepted the view Hayek and Keynes shared that ideas have great power to change the world for good or ill, even if that power is sometimes slow to take effect.

In 2004, an article by Diana Bagnall in *The Bulletin*, Australia's main news magazine, described me as the 'most influential man in Australia', saying that the Centre had 'its fingerprints … all over this country's political agenda, on both sides'. Not bad, I guess, for an intellectual entrepreneur. Many of the ideas we've had about what governments should do and what individuals should do for themselves have increasingly become general practice in the past 30 years, but there is still a lengthy agenda of work ahead. The CIS exists to underpin the free society and its liberal democratic institutions. But it is a troubled world – I cannot see us being able to rest on our laurels any time soon. Australia and New Zealand are free and prosperous nations and Australia's economic performance in the last decade or so has outpaced that of much of the world, but the intellectual and policy wins that we have achieved can easily be reversed unless they are continually reinforced. Free trade, for instance, is subject to the whims of politicians and voters, and has always been so. Where those whims turn next will to some extent determine where we have to act to inform and guide the environment of ideas.

3 BRAZIL: A CONTRAST OF IDEAS
Margaret Tse, Instituto Liberdade (Brazil)

Introduction

The history of Brazil suggests that dominant ideas have always had a profound influence on social and political issues. This chapter explains why the adoption and promotion of free market ideas could be especially powerful at moments of particularly rapid change and acute confusion, shaping human experience over time and underpinning the intellectual capital of the country. The Instituto Liberdade is playing a crucial role in influencing the climate of ideas in the contemporary scene.

Historical roots from Portuguese colonisation

Many elements of the Portuguese colonisation are deeply rooted in the fabric of Brazilian society. To properly explore these roots, it may be useful to go back in history. History professor José Murilo de Carvalho (2000: 8) theorises that the legacy of slavery has infected contemporary Brazilian society such that many people often consider themselves above the law. Slavery was introduced shortly after the conquest of the land by the Portuguese in 1500 and lasted for more than three hundred years until it was abolished in 1888 after Brazil became an independent country. Research shows that around four million slaves, about 34 per cent of the total African slaves transported to the Americas, were brought to Brazil over the course of three centuries. Slavery was rooted in Brazil's social practices and value system. Clearly, at this time, individual freedom was not seen as a relevant social value.

The widespread emphasis on exploitation within Brazilian society was visible through the dominance of the large landed estates. The unequal and irregular distribution and occupation of land started in the sixteenth century, when the Portuguese crown conceded vast 'captaincies' to early colonists as a reward for services and, later on, for joining forces with the local oligarchies to maintain power. According to Carvalho, unlike the situation in the colonies of North America, there was no family farming in Brazil and landowners were slave-owners (ibid.). Even with the introduction of a land law which allowed the importation of free workers from Europe, the social and political impact of the *latifundia* (landed estates) was deep rooted. Landlords exploited their tenants' labour and, after democracy arrived, harvested their votes.

Patrimonialism, a type of rule in which the ruler does not distinguish between personal and public authority and treats matters and resources of state as his personal affair, was another major component of the Portuguese state and society during the country's conquest of Brazil. Portugal lacked the manpower to rule and explore the immense empire it had conquered, so it appointed the ruling class to the administration of the colony and this became a defining characteristic of the colonial government. Carvalho suggests that a lack of strong civil society and the large number of Brazilians incorporated into the colony's bureaucracy, compounded by clientelism and nepotism, contributed to the survival of patrimonial traits in present day Brazil (ibid.).

After fifteen years of democratic rule, the widespread prevalence and tolerance of corruption – a consequence of patrimonial and clientelistic practices – is expressed through a high degree of impunity.

The combination of the indigenous Brazilians' lack of need for a plan, the Portuguese desire for quick enrichment, and the slaves' inability to own or invest in anything, formed the culture of today.

Moreover, Carvalho (2005) states that corruption is deeply rooted in the contemporary leftist Workers' Party in the country, not as a vulgar way for personal money-making, but as a technical instrument to erode the moral basis of capitalistic society and to fund the socialist revolutionary strategy. These two objectives are closely intertwined. Funded by corruption, the growth of leftist parties strengthens the credibility of the attacks they make against society. Capitalism would not appear so immoral without their deliberate efforts to degrade moral standards.

The influence of positivism and its fallacies

The concept of positivism, conceived by French philosopher Auguste Comte (1798–1857), influenced large parts of Latin America during the nineteenth century and was adopted by the military, technocratic and political elites in Brazil. In 1889, the republicans coined the phrase 'Order and Progress', which is still emblazoned on the Brazilian flag today. The goal of progress in this case was a 'socially responsible authoritarianism' which could provide 'scientific solutions' for society's problems.

According to Zimmermann (2007), 'Positivists argued that only such a "scientific" government could generate high levels of national development, thereby supporting the "moral" superiority of dictatorship over constitutional democracy. In Brazil, the disciples of Comte were involved, decisively, in the overthrow of the monarchy in the hope that this would be succeeded by a dictatorial republic.'

Comte postulated an empirical science-based view of sociology and believed that an appreciation of the past, and the ability to build upon it towards the future, was crucial in transitioning from the theological and metaphysical phases.

Austrian economist Ludwig von Mises (1985) explains:

> The sciences of human action start from the fact that man purposefully aims at ends he has chosen. It is precisely this that all brands of positivism, behaviorism, and panphysicalism want either to deny altogether or to pass over in silence … All that 'Unified Science' brought forward was to recommend the proscription of the methods applied by the sciences of human action and their replacement by the methods of the experimental natural sciences. It is not remarkable for that which it contributed, but only for that which it wants to see prohibited. Its protagonists are the champions of intolerance and of a narrow-minded dogmatism.

Mueller (2002) describes the effects in Brazil:

> Comte's ideas have shown their greatest impact in economic policy. Given the facts that members of the military have played a central role in Brazil's political life and that positivism had become the leading philosophical paradigm at the military schools, economic policy in Brazil has been marked by an interventionist frenzy that affects all aspects of public life. The spirit of planning for modernity has

turned Brazil into a hotbed of economic interventionism,
with each new government promising the great leap forward.

Gramsci's hegemony theory

The Italian communist leader Antonio Gramsci (1891–1937) was
a highly unique Marxist who was concerned about what strategies should be adopted by revolutionary parties operating in
liberal democratic states. This led him to analyse the relationship
between the economic base and the political superstructure and
to introduce the concept of hegemony. Power, which is so deeply
desired, must exist in a twofold nature: one formal and objective,
essentially structural like the state, and the other more impre-
cise and abstract, with a conjectural basis relative to civil society.
Coutinho (2002) states that in order to grasp power, as described
in Gramsci's concepts, it is imperative to grasp hegemony first and
make social institutions mere mechanisms of party propaganda,
thereby destroying society from the inside in a slow but mortal
attack to all forms of resistance.

Costa (2004) adds,

> Gramsci's concern with revolutionary violence is not moral,
> but instrumental. His complementary strategy of war of
> position – trench warfare – uses a lot of violent resources
> previously used by orthodox revolutionaries, such as
> misinformation, ideological manipulation of the masses,
> enlarging State (in an advanced stage of the revolution)
> and, at last, rupture, which would not refuse, if necessary,
> traditional violence as the last fatal and efficient strike.

Brazil is possibly the only country in the world where Gramsci's strategy is in an advanced position. Staying above the

competition among political representatives was the left's strategy for maintaining its hegemonic position. Today, Brazil does not have any political opposition to facilitate any plurality of ideas.

According to Carvalho (2005), a well-planned and highly successful scheme aiming at establishing a communist regime has been under way in Brazil since 1964. In all sectors of the government, as well as in the Congress and Houses of Representatives of all 26 states and in about five thousand municipalities of the country, most politicians came from former leftist movements, many of them ex-terrorists, including high-ranking officials. The 'São Paulo Forum' (SPF), founded in 1990 by Fidel Castro and current President Lula, is the strategic headquarters of the Latin American revolutionary left. Their ultimate goal is to establish a dictatorship of one party, with absolute power in their hands and complete restriction of any demonstration of individualism, with the intent to resort to violence in order to reach their goals of socialising the country. Carvalho stresses that this revolutionary mentality is totalitarian and violent in itself because the imposition of ever more suffocating restrictions to human liberty has been combined with the dissemination of the revolutionary mentality among ever growing segments of the population.

Costa (2004) continues,

> What denounces the Gramscian revolution even more is that in Brazil, individual conscience is slowly being substituted by the concept of the political correctness and moral relativism. Examples of this abound: armed members of MST [Landless People´s Movement] who invade farms are victims and farmers who defend themselves are criminals; drug-dealers who are provoking a civil war in Rio de Janeiro are victims of the system, and if they are found guilty, we, law-enforcing

citizens, must share that guilt a bit (as the media informs us every day); priests who speak up against abortion and homosexuality are children-devouring monsters, but friars who embraced liberation theology and say that Cuba is paradise on Earth – no matter the 17,000 murdered – are portrayed as the highest models of Christianity.

Rule of law versus rules of society

Brazilian social institutions are subject to two types of pressure. One is the universal pressure that comes from the bureaucratic norms and laws that define the existence of public service. The other is determined based on the webs of personal relations to which all are subjected and by the social resources that these networks mobilise and distribute. Brazil has a deep relationship-based society.

In Latin American countries such as Brazil, 'Constitutions typically contain a substantial number of aspirational or utopian provisions that are either impossible or extremely difficult to enforce. Some of these provisions contain social rights that seem far more appropriate in a political platform or a sermon than in a constitution' (Rosenn, 1990).

Brazil is a typical example of a country where the 'laws' of the society can easily overrule the laws of the state. DaMatta (1999) has argued that Brazilian society is pervaded by a 'double ethic', because methods for circumventing state laws can be obtained through a range of factors related to conditions of wealth, social status, family ties and friendship. Legalism in Brazil is the result of the problematic legacy of a convoluted legal system introduced by the Portuguese colonisers. Brazilians have acquired a certain tendency to soften laws by not applying them properly. As a result, we observe a chaotic and insecure environment for entrepreneurs.

Many of Brazil's national afflictions, such as crippling taxes, red tape, land invasions, endemic corruption throughout all levels of government and in all three branches of the country, lack of infrastructure and an unreliable judicial system, all contribute to the crowding out of enterprise or cause it to be driven underground. Everyone talks about wanting honest politicians, but few Brazilians complain about the size of the government, in spite of the creation of a tax meter by the São Paulo Chamber of Commerce, which tots up the government's tax rate in real time. Instituto Liberdade uses this meter to create awareness when celebrating Tax Freedom Day (the first day of the year in which a nation as a whole has theoretically earned enough income to fund its annual tax burden) in Brazil.

As Schor (2006) explains, 'constitutions are not entrenched in Latin America because political leaders do not fear citizen mobilization when fundamental rules of the game are violated'. In general, Congress ignores the problems of the people that it represents and legislators are rarely held accountable to voters or their party and are granted widespread immunity from prosecution. We also have a judiciary that administers the laws according to the power and the influence of the lawyers and the personal relationships between the interested parties. If the proposed reforms of Brazil's political, fiscal, judicial, social security and labour systems are achieved, it would solve the problems that we have with violence, property rights violations, poor public education, chaos within the healthcare system, the environment, government inefficiency and corruption.

The problem is that there is an absence of authentic classical liberal political parties. Classical liberalism, that is limited governments, free trade and private institutions apart from the state, is not present in politics today – not even in the form of a campaign promise. Classical liberalism has very few academic spokesmen in the country and the ones that do exist lack the political support to be able to offer attractive platform proposals that appeal to the intellectual and emotional sides of Brazilians.

Classical liberalism in Brazil was pioneered by Donald Stewart, Jr. A businessman and civil engineer, he translated *Human Action* by Mises into Portuguese and wrote articles and books about liberal thought. In order to persuade Brazilian society of the advantages of a liberal order he founded the Instituto Liberal in 1983, in Rio de Janeiro. Although he passed away in 1999, his efforts and dedication to the cause changed the minds of future generations of intellectual entrepreneurs, who continued the work of promoting the ideas and expanding the debates.

Currently, there are few free market think tanks in Brazil and the most active ones are located in the southern regions of the country. The freedom fighters from the state of Rio Grande do Sul are typically descended from working-class European settlers and are characterised by their strong tradition of classical liberal values. In 1835, the overtaxation of beef jerky, the state's main source of revenue at that time, by the Portuguese crown, angered local farmers and cattle raisers tied to the Freemasons, sparking an uprising called the Farroupilha Revolution. This was very similar to the Boston Tea Party in the USA, which sparked the American Revolution. The war lasted for ten years and ended with the defeat of the rebels. The revolution did not result in the state of Rio Grande do Sul becoming an independent country, but the traditional classical liberal spirit continues to live on.

This essay focuses on how ideas have impacted on Brazil, and also how the work of Instituto Liberdade, a small and independent free market think tank located in the southern region, is gradually affecting civil society by reaching out to intellectuals, teachers and entrepreneurs. Its continuous efforts over the course of 21 years in researching and analysing public policy issues, publishing free market literature and organising colloquiums and seminars show the dedication of Brazilian intellectual entrepreneurs to bringing their insights to the attention of policymakers, opinion leaders and the media. In order to promote a better political, economic and cultural environment in such a big and diverse country, the Institute is returning to its roots and engaging with the country's challenges directly, in the belief that the population is resourceful and capable of spontaneous creativity based on free market ideas. One of the objectives of the Institute is to continue producing academic studies, but no longer limited to the field of economics. By putting a greater focus on Aristotle's ideas of natural order and the political science based on the ideas of philosophers from the Age of Enlightenment – that is, where the law exists to serve justice and the state is not the only source of answers – we could develop a more positive approach towards liberal democracy, and more specifically a more truly democratic government that follows the rule of law, emphasising the protection of rights and freedoms of individuals from government power.

We hope that in the near future the country will reflect the predictions of John Blundell, Director General, and Ralph Harris, Fellow, at the Institute of Economic Affairs:

Massively rising expectations, greater knowledge, growing life expectancy, failing public enterprises, continuous improvement in the private sector, falling voter turnout, failing parties, growing pressure groups: these are all powerful trends, but together they add up to a monumental sea-change. The politicians who embrace these changes and work with them will be the ones my great grandchildren will read about in modern history, say 50 years from now. (Blundell, 2007: 132–3)

References

Blundell, J. (2007), *Waging the War of Ideas*, 3rd edn, London: Institute of Economic Affairs.

Carvalho, J. M. de (2000), *The Struggle for Democracy in Brazil: Possible Lessons for Nigeria*, Amsterdam/Port Harcourt: SEPHIS and the University of Port Harcourt.

Carvalho, O. de (2005), 'Brazilian left: from victory to defeat to victory again', Presentation delivered at the Atlas Economic Research Foundation Seminar, 18 September.

Costa, J. (2004), 'Gramsci's violence in Brazil', *Mídia Sem Máscara*, 25 May.

Coutinho, S. A. de A. (2002), *A revolução Gramscista no ocidente* (The Gramscist Revolution in the West), Rio de Janeiro: Estandarte Editora.

DaMatta, R. A. (1987), 'The quest for citizenship in a relational universe', in *State and Society in Brazil: Continuity and Change*, Boulder, CO: Westview Press, pp. 318–19.

DaMatta, R. A. (1991), *Carnivals, Rogues, and Heroes: An Interpretation of the Brazilian Dilemma*, Notre Dame, IN: University of Notre Dame Press, pp. 187–8.

DaMatta, R. A. (1999), 'Is Brazil hopelessly corrupt?', in *The Brazil Reader: History, Culture, Politics*, Durham, NC: Duke University Press, p. 295.

Fausto, B. (1977), 'O Brasil republicano', in *História geral da civilização brasileira*, São Paulo: Difel, vol. 3, p. 138.

Hardy, H. (2006), *Isaiah Berlin's Political Ideas in the Romantic Age*, Princeton, NJ: Princeton University Press.

Mises, L. v. (1978), *The Ultimate Foundation of Economic Science: An Essay on Method*, Kansas City, KS: Sheed Andrews and McMeel, p. 122.

Mises, L. v. (1985), *Theory and History*, Washington, DC: Ludwig von Mises Institute, pp. 3–226.

Mueller, A. P. (2002), *The Ghost that Haunts Brazil*, Auburn, VA: Ludwig von Mises Institute.

Rosenn, K. S. (1990), 'The success of constitutionalism in the United States and its failure in Latin America: an explanation', *University of Miami Inter-American Law Review*, vol. 22.

Rosenn, K. S. (1998), *O jeito na cultura jurídica brasileira*, Rio de Janeiro: Renovar, p. 528.

Schor, M. (2006), 'Constitutionalism through the looking glass of Latin America', *Texas International Law Journal*, 1: 20.

Tse, M. (2007), *Hostile Environment in Brazil for Entrepreneurs*, Porto Alegre: Instituto Liberdade.

Véliz, C. (1980), *The Centralist Tradition of Latin America*, Princeton, NJ: Princeton University Press, p. 195.

Zea, L. (1980), *Pensamiento positivista latinoamericano*, Caracas: Biblioteca Ayacucho.

Zimmermann, A. (2006), 'The left-wing threat to Brazil's democracy', *National Observer* (*Council for the National Interest*), 68: 48–54.

Zimmermann, A. (2007), 'Legal and extra-legal obstacles for the realization of the Rule of Law in Brazil', *Murdoch University Electronic Journal of Law* (E-Law), 14(1).

4 IF IT MATTERS, MEASURE IT
Michael Walker, Fraser Institute (Canada)

Let's go get them

The Fraser Institute was founded in 1974 by Canadian industrialist T. P. Boyle with the advice of his colleague, economist and former Hungarian freedom fighter Csaba Hajdu, and by the direct efforts of Sally Pipes, John Raybould and Michael Walker. The two main differences that characterised the Fraser Institute's approach and its publications from other policy think tanks of the era were the empirical focus on very specific public policy issues of the day and an attention to marketing the studies to the broadest possible audience. The former attribute reflected my training as an econometrician, the latter the incredible energy and 'let's go get them' attitude of John Raybould and Sally Pipes. In particular, in the words of John Raybould, the Fraser Institute tried to lower the 'fog index' associated with its publications so that they would be accessible to the widest possible audience. (It is interesting to note that when he left the Fraser Institute to return to the United Kingdom because of family issues, John Raybould went to work for the Institute of Economic Affairs (IEA), where his job was the marketing of IEA publications.) Later we were fortunate to attract to our staff the libertarian *Übermensch* Walter Block, who for ten years was the dominant libertarian in Canada.

People are not entitled to their own facts

We rely primarily on measurement because we recognise that disputes about public policies are often based on opinions that have been formed without a careful consideration of all the facts. While everyone is entitled to their own opinions, they are not entitled to their own facts. It was and is our view at the Fraser Institute that, perhaps not immediately but in the end, many disputes about public policy can be resolved by the infusion of a generally agreed upon set of facts.

If it matters, measure it

The Institute's motto, 'if it matters, measure it', also reflects the belief that through a programme of careful measurement an institute can change the agenda of public discussion. Of course, the measurements have to be relevant and have to be related in some way to an interest that ordinary citizens have in a particular outcome. For this reason, we often say that the Institute's job is to think ahead a number of years to the public policy issues that will occupy the minds of the public and be ready with a publication that takes advantage of this natural demand for information, thus changing the public's view of that topic. The strategic idea here is that it is easier to fulfil a demand for information that already exists than it is to create a demand for that information and then to fulfil it.

In the beginning

This forward-looking approach will only work, however, if the topic of concern is projected into the public's eye by the natural course of events. So, for example, the first book that the Institute published dealt with the problems that rent controls would produce for tenants. We knew that, in a very short period of time, the existence of rent control would make it more difficult for tenants to find lodgings and that this would produce a demand for information about the rent controls themselves. Our assessment was accurate and *Rent Control – A Popular Paradox* became a national bestseller in Canada and found its way onto book racks in corner stores.

Our second book, *The Illusion of Wage and Price Controls*, was also a bestseller, and for the same reasons. Both books had the effect of destroying the credibility of the policy they targeted. In the case of wage and price controls, our book helped mobilise the trade union movement in Canada to fight wage controls.

The key challenge – getting a share of the public's mind

By far the toughest job that public policy research institutes have to do is to create awareness about a public policy issue that has not already attracted public attention. Most citizens do not wake up in the morning asking themselves, 'I wonder what public policy is doing today?' The fact that most citizens are more focused on their own lives and parochial concerns explains why politicians often use emotional arguments and exaggerated claims to attract the interest of the public to their political position. Since public policy organisations are trying to encourage citizens to be more rational in their approach to public policy questions, it is obvious why we are often fighting an ineffectual rearguard action.

Measure what matters to the public

Having recognised this problem at an early stage in its development, the Fraser Institute has adopted a different strategy from most public policy organisations in approaching the problem of mobilising opinion. Rather than reprinting classic masters like Frédéric Bastiat, Adam Smith and Friedrich Hayek, the Institute, as noted, sought to publish current economic analysis on topics related to pressing policy issues that were already in the public focus. But we also set out to provide measurements for public consumption that would address a deeper policy concern by mobilising citizens' concerns about their own wallet or other direct impacts on their family circumstances.

One of the earliest projects of this kind undertaken by the Institute was the creation of the Consumer Tax Index and the associated calculation of Tax Freedom Day. The idea of the Consumer Tax Index emerged from the observation that consumers had a natural interest in how much they were paying for the goods and services they consumed and the monthly release of the government's consumer price index resulted in a lot of comments in the media. There was, however, almost no discussion of the cost of public services that were being consumed and the attendant tax burdens required to finance them.

Like how many days do *you* work for the government?

The Consumer Tax Index calculations were begun in 1976 and continue to be one of the most successful projects in the Institute's history. The annual studies that are required to produce the index include: calculation of the tax burden borne by families at different income levels; a comparison of the tax burdens in different provinces; a comparison of the tax burden with the cost of the necessities of life and how these comparisons have changed since 1961, the earliest date for which calculations can be made. The results of the tax studies make it possible to calculate Tax Freedom Day, the day in the year when the citizen with average income has worked long enough to pay the full tax bill owing to the various levels of government.

Tax Freedom Day has become one of the most widely known statistical facts in the country. The once obtuse provisions of federal and provincial budgets are now all reduced to the simple question, 'Will Tax Freedom Day be earlier in the year or later in the year?' During 2006 there were 475 media stories using Tax Freedom Day and the information contained in the *Tax Facts* book, which every other year compiles the calculations made to produce the Consumer Tax Index and Tax Freedom Day.

Become a 'go to' source for relevant information

Apart from the direct media impact effect upon the climate of opinion, the Institute's work on taxation has made it a 'go to' source of information on a wide variety of topics related to government activities. As a consequence, the Fraser Institute is regarded within Canada as the most important force pushing governments to adopt a more conservative stance on public finances and the control of public expenditure. In Canada, the Fraser Institute is synonymous with fiscal probity, lower taxes and responsible fiscal conduct.

One of the spin-offs of our work on taxation and public expenditure has been the publication of our annual report cards on the tax, spending and debt management of the ten provincial governments and the federal government. These report cards are now so widely used by the public in Canada – particularly by those deciding whether or not to purchase government bonds – that even socialist governments within the country use their rating on the Fraser Institute's scorecard as a way of promoting their province when their score is good. A poor showing on a report card often produces telephone calls from provincial premiers and ministers of finance complaining that they have not been understood or that their position has in some way been misrepresented.

Measure the economic freedom of the world

It is often said that success begets success. This is the case with the Fraser Institute's focus on measurement as a way of achieving public policy objectives. Having observed the huge success of our tax measurement studies and Tax Freedom Day, the Institute began to apply the same strategy in other areas of public policy. One of the most outstanding results has been the Economic Freedom of the World Index.

In 1986, following a conference on the relationship between economic, civil and political freedom, the Fraser Institute decided, with the help of Liberty Fund Inc., to launch a programme of study and discussion that would lead to the construction of a global index of economic freedom. The objective was to raise the level of discussion of economic freedom by journalists, politicians and the general public, by providing a league table that would make the concept of economic freedom more tangible. By 1986, we had had a decade of experience of raising the level of public discussion of fiscal issues using a variety of derivatives from the Canadian Consumer Tax Index. It was my hope that we would be able to accomplish for discussion of economic freedom what we had already done for the discussion of fiscal affairs. While we are a long way from achieving a satisfactory level of economic freedom around the world, there can be no question that the Economic Freedom of the World Index has made a material difference in raising the level of economic freedom. It has been effective, in part, because of the creation of the Economic Freedom of the World Network: a network of institutes in nearly eighty countries which collaborate annually in the publication and release of the Index. Some of the members of the network have followed the Fraser Institute's lead and have created sub-national indices of economic freedom so as to encourage the discussion of variations between sub-national units such as provinces. Notable examples are India, China and Argentina.

Find out what families are concerned about and measure it

While the Fraser Institute has been quite aggressive in using the economic freedom of the world methodology to encourage greater levels of economic freedom in Canada, it has also been using a variety of other measurements that have had a significant impact on public policy. While the constraints of the space available in this essay make it impossible to provide anything like a complete list of these projects, in the space remaining I will provide two examples that can be readily adapted to other countries.

Undoubtedly, the building of human capital is the most important aspect of both personal success and the prosperity of a nation. The development of human capital begins in the education system, yet it is an unfortunate reality that in most countries of the world this most crucial 'industry' is entirely owned by the government and funded by block grants from government. In many instances, this state education apparatus does not perform well and does not produce the kinds of additions to human capital that are commensurate with the large amounts of money which are spent to support it.

Notwithstanding this fact, in most countries the majority believe that the public education system is absolutely essential. The role of public policy research organisations is twofold: on one hand, they must document the quality of the public education system, and on the other hand, they must give an indication of the benefits of private education. A tremendously powerful tool for accomplishing both these goals is the creation and wide dissemination of report cards on the performance of public and private schools.

Measure schools' performance and millions will pay attention

In 1998, the Fraser Institute began a project whose long-term goal is to publish comprehensive report cards on every high school in every Canadian province for which data is available. Currently, the Institute publishes evaluations of 5,700 high schools that provide education to 3 million children. These report cards have had a dramatic impact on the education debate and the choices that parents have been making about where to send their children for schooling.

The strategy behind the school report card programme is similar to that discussed above. Parents have a natural interest in the welfare of their children and a curiosity about the quality of the schools they attend. The report cards feed this natural demand for information.

Media compete to publish the league tables

The media have been quick to realise the interest that parents and grandparents have in the performance of schools. Consequently, in every jurisdiction where we are able to produce a report card, we have a media partner. The partner is usually a newspaper, but sometimes it is a news magazine, and it reports the results of the report card analysis. The media outlet also uses this as an opportunity to run a series of stories about education and a comparison of school performance. This comparative study, together with the reporting of the performance results, has made the annual release of the results of the school report cards the most important public policy development in education during the year.

In fact, the news magazine *L'Actualité* in Quebec, which has one of the widest circulations in that province, dedicates more than eighty pages of a special annual edition of its magazine to the report cards. Reader surveys by the magazine have ascertained that more than a million citizens read the results and use them as a means for assessing the quality of education. A competing publication, not sympathetic to the idea of assessing school performance, did, however, note that enrolment in private schools had increased by 30 per cent as a consequence of the wide availability of these measures.

But the most important effect that the report cards have had is to make school performance an issue for teachers, administrators, politicians and, most importantly, the parents of the pupils. In some provinces, such as British Columbia, the government has responded to the performance measures by enabling parents to cross enrolment boundaries to take advantage of schools that are better than the ones in the neighbourhoods where they live. As can be imagined, this combination has produced increased pressure on the state school system and made performance enhancement more important for school administrators.

Measure hospital waiting lists and change public opinion about the public health monopoly

A second area where the measurement of public services performance has had a beneficial effect is in healthcare. Seventeen years ago, realising that the public ownership and operation of the healthcare system, and a lack of pricing signals to users, would lead to shortages and rationing, the Fraser Institute began a programme of measuring hospital waiting lists. These measurements have shaped the debate and mobilised public opinion about the adequacy of the current healthcare system in Canada.

Most importantly, the waiting list measures have generated thousands of newspaper and television stories and have facilitated a general acceptance of the idea that the public healthcare system, as it exists now, has been failing citizens. Correspondingly, when the Supreme Court of Canada was asked to consider the case of a citizen who had waited a very long time for hip surgery, it concluded that the healthcare system as it presently operates is not answering the needs of citizens and that the prohibition of the purchase of private healthcare in Canada is a violation of their constitutional rights. These Supreme Court decisions have served to define the future outline of the discussion of healthcare in Canada and will undoubtedly lead to an increased reliance on private care and to less confidence in a monopoly public system.

5 THE BATTLE OF IDEAS IN CHILE: THE CASE OF LIBERTAD Y DESARROLLO

Cristián Larroulet, Libertad y Desarrollo (Chile)

Introduction

This chapter describes the key importance of ideas – and the institutions that promote them – in Chile's political, economic and social development.

During the 1960s and early 1970s, Chile was known for taking significant steps towards the socialist model. This process culminated in a severe economic, social and political crisis, leading to a virtual state of civil war. Thirty years later, however, Chile has transformed its economy in the direction of a free market system, opened its markets to the world, and advanced the welfare of its inhabitants (Buchi, 1993). It is also recognised as an example of a well-established democracy and a successful political transition from a military regime (which lasted for sixteen years).

Friedrich Hayek noted long ago that 'the only way to change the course of society is to change its ideas' (Blundell, 2004). Chile is a good illustration. Half a century ago, an agreement between the University of Chicago's Institute of Economics and Santiago's Catholic University brought free market ideas into Chile with clarity and force. In the generations that followed, these ideas were transmitted to economists, entrepreneurs, journalists and intellectuals, who have successfully influenced public policy (Rosende, 2007). Thanks to the work of other universities and research centres these ideas are gaining broad support and continue to be highly influential in contributing to the level of social and economic development in Chile (Larroulet, 2003).

The first part of this chapter describes the transformation process in Chile, specifically its free market reforms and their consequences. The second section describes the experiences of Libertad y Desarrollo (LyD), a research and educational centre which, since the completion of Chile's transition to democracy in 1990, has consistently promoted free market ideas steeped in the tradition of thinkers such as Friedrich Hayek, Milton Friedman and Gary Becker. The paper concludes by noting key lessons from Chile's experience in promoting ideas in favour of a free society.

I have had the personal good fortune of being closely involved in this experience of national transformation, which some have called revolutionary (Tironi, 2002). After attending Chile's Pontifical Catholic University in the 1970s, in the 1980s I studied at the University of Chicago's Department of Economics, where George Stigler, Gary Becker and Arnold Harberger were among my professors. Later, I served in the Chilean ministries of economy and finance and helped to design and implement reforms in areas such as privatisation, competition, trade liberalisation, tax reduction and social programmes for the needy. In combination with many other initiatives, these policies contributed to Chile's transformation from a socialist economy to a market economy and ultimately allowed the country to reach its current level of development. Finally, I had the opportunity to serve as Executive Director of Libertad y Desarrollo and help the think tank to promote public policies based on the ideas of a free society. As a result, over the past 27 years I have had the privilege of witnessing the impact of ideas on a country's transition process. I have also been able to affirm the importance of liberty. The rule of law, private property, free trade, competition and an auxiliary role for the state, among other factors, are essential conditions for development.

From a socialist country to a free society

During the second half of the nineteenth century, Chile was one of the most prosperous countries in Latin America. This situation was the result of many years of political stability, clear institutional rules and a functioning market economy which was relatively open to the global marketplace. Within the political sphere, the ideas of the rule of law and republican ideology had been promoted by distinguished leaders such as Minister Diego Portales, President Manuel Montt and lawmaker Andrés Bello. Within the economic field, the French economist Jean Gustave Courcelle-Seneuil, who embraced the ideas of Adam Smith, was a powerful supporter of free trade in Chile (Couyoumdjian, 2008). He was also extremely influential in his capacity as adviser to the Chilean government, and taught economics at the University of Chile.

Beginning in the early twentieth century, however, nationalist and socialist ideas gradually gained influence among policymakers, pushing them in the direction of greater state intervention. This process was accelerated by the depression of the 1930s, which severely affected Chile. Between 1929 and 1932, GDP decreased by 45 per cent. The impact of the crisis was dramatic, and, as is often seen in such circumstances, public opinion shifted towards greater state involvement and protectionism. Confidence in the private sector fell. Interventionist policies gained greater acceptance among the public and were viewed as necessary remedies. The so-called 'import substitution model', advocated by the Economic Commission for Latin America and the Caribbean (ECLAC), exerted a strong influence on policy. Import duties were systematically raised and numerous barriers to trade were introduced.

At first, increased protectionism and interventionist government policies resulted in growth in production. But the subsequent poor allocation of resources, lack of competition and low productivity rapidly diminished Chile's rate of economic growth. Prevailing socialist attitudes blamed individuals and the private sector for these failures, however, and insisted that there needed to be even more radical policies for increasing state involvement in the production and regulation of goods and services. Meanwhile, the higher public spending levels that resulted from this interventionism raised the tax burden and put an additional brake on the economy. The process culminated with the reappearance of high inflation rates.

In 1970, for the first time in Chile's history, a Marxist-socialist president, Salvador Allende, took office as President of the Republic. Allende attempted to convert Chile into a socialist economy and placed most of the country's productive and service sectors into state hands. He continued to close the economy even further, and through a huge increase in public spending produced a massive macroeconomic imbalance (Meller and Larrain, 1991). The resulting political, economic and social chaos led to a state of civil conflict which the country's political leaders were unable to control. In September 1973, a military coup put an end to Chilean democracy.

The armed forces lacked confidence in the political class, which they held responsible for the crisis that had brought the military to power. They also lacked the economic expertise necessary to manage problems such as hyperinflation, food shortages, the falling investment rate and the balance of payments crisis. As a result, they placed their trust in a group of economists schooled in classical liberal thought.

Many of these experts had studied at the University of Chicago and were associated with Chile's two leading universities: the University of Chile and the Catholic University. They had been educated in the tradition of Frank Knight, Theodore Schultz, Harry Johnson, Milton Friedman and George Stigler. In response to the crisis situation of the early 1970s, they had prepared a manifesto now known as *El Ladrillo* (The Brick) (De Castro, 1992), which outlined the key economic and social reforms they considered necessary to end the crisis. This group, nicknamed the 'Chicago Boys', instituted a set of radical reforms to re-establish fiscal equilibrium, control inflation, open the economy by reducing tariffs and eliminating non-tariff barriers, and free prices in all markets except monopolistic sectors. The markets for capital and labour were liberalised and made more flexible. Numerous barriers to entry, which had restricted competition, were eliminated. Reforms were also carried out to allow private sector participation in a wide range of areas, including energy, telecommunications, basic and higher education and pension fund administration.

Another notable achievement by the Chicago Boys was groundbreaking reform in the area of social programmes, which, in general, had not effectively served the poor (Larroulet, 1993). In response to this situation, policies were prioritised in favour of employment. Housing programmes, healthcare, retirement insurance, education and monetary subsidies were targeted towards the most needy.

Of course, errors were made in the implementation of some of these reforms, but the final result was a profound transformation of the Chilean economy from a socialist-statist model to a more free market system.

These transformations were carried out amid sharp criticism from groups opposed to the military government, most notably all members of the leftist and centre-left political parties. Thus, there was still widespread doubt in the late 1980s about the stability and viability of these reforms over the long run. This doubt was further reinforced when the reforms, owing to internal errors as well as external factors arising from the economic and financial crisis that plagued Latin America during the 1980s, were unable to show clear results in the form of increased wellbeing for the population. It should be noted that during this period per capita income fell by an average of 0.9 per cent per year in Latin America, leading many to refer to the 1980s as 'the lost decade'. This situation, which also affected Chile, did not promote the acceptance of free market reforms within Chilean society.

The transition to democracy began in 1988, when the military government lost a plebiscite, calling a presidential election in 1989. The victor in this election was Patricio Aylwin, the candidate of the centre-left coalition called the Concertación. The transition process involved negotiations and agreements between the military government and the new authorities, most notably the consensual reforms to the Constitution of the Republic. The minister of the interior at that time, Carlos Cáceres, played a particularly noteworthy role in this process.[1]

The candidate with the second-largest percentage of the vote during the 1989 elections was Hernán Büchi. Having held several

---

1   Currently chairman of the board of Libertad y Desarrollo; member of the Mont Pèlerin Society and former minister of finance, 1983.

public offices, including minister of finance from 1985 to 1989, Büchi worked to reorient the country's economic policies in the direction of the free market. It is important to recall that in the years previous to his economic leadership, the country had experienced a severe crisis, leading to a 14 per cent drop in GDP in 1982 and an unemployment rate above 15 per cent in 1984. However, under Büchi's management Chile enjoyed an annual GDP growth rate of 8 per cent and unemployment was reduced to about 6 per cent by 1989.

Intellectual entrepreneurs: the case of Libertad y Desarrollo (LyD)
An 'enterprise of ideas' is born

As previously mentioned, many of the economists and politicians of the new democratic administration in 1990 had been highly critical of most of the free market reforms implemented under the military government. Additionally, many free market supporters feared that the new authorities would return to the failed policies of the past. The idea arose to create a 'think tank' that would vigorously defend and promote public policies based on the principles of a free society. Thus a group of people assembled by Hernán Büchi set out to create Libertad y Desarrollo.[2] The new institution was defined as a study and research centre specialising in public policies which was independent of any political, religious or commercial affiliation.

---

2   The first board consisted of Hernán Büchi, Carlos F. Cáceres, Ernesto Illanes, Patricia Matte, Ricardo Rivadeneira, Lucía Santa Cruz and Eugenio Valenzuela. The initial executive team was Luis Larraín, Denise Couyoumdjian, Manuel Cereceda and Pablo Ihnen.

The organisation was founded on three strategic pillars. The first, which is encompassed in its mission statement, is to defend the principles of a free society; that is, to promote individual freedom and to make individuals the central focus of public policy – in other words, democracy, market economy, rule of law and limited government. The second pillar is the development of strong technical expertise in identifying problem areas and designing public policies that will contribute to the country's development in the broadest sense of the word. This calls for significant investment in human capital in order to assemble experts who can address these tasks with the speed and rigour demanded by the rapidly evolving public debate. The third strategic pillar is the development of close ties with the leading institutions involved in the formulation of public policies. In other words, in order to have influence over public policy, it is necessary to establish direct relationships with the government, Congress, the judicial branch, the political parties, the communications media, the universities and other relevant institutions of civil society.

We began our work in March 1990 with a team of eight professionals. Our staff currently includes 29 experts from the political, economic, social, environmental and legal fields – all of whom are highly influential within the public policy debate in Chile. It is sufficient to note that during 2007, Libertad y Desarrollo or its researchers were cited on average more than 9.8 times per day in the media. Its website, www.lyd.org, has become one of the most visited in Latin America, and over 600,000 copies of its reports and studies are distributed each year. While approximately forty people currently work at the institute, LyD has made significant long-term investments in human capital over the past eighteen years, including supporting twenty young professionals in postgraduate studies at leading universities abroad.

From the start we were determined to develop close relations with think tanks in other countries that shared our concern for defending the ideas of a free society. Thus, we quickly became involved in the activities of the Atlas Economic Research Foundation, the Heritage Foundation and the Cato Institute in the United States; Canada's Fraser Institute; the Institute of Economic Affairs in England; and many others. We also decided that our institution should have a complementary profile to that of the already prestigious Centro de Estudios Públicos (CEP), which was founded in Chile in the early 1980s and had been extremely influential in spreading classical liberal ideas. In contrast to the work of the CEP, however, LyD's efforts are focused on the daily battle over specific public policies.

In addition to our work in Chile over the past eighteen years, we have undertaken a large number of international efforts, including contributing to seminars organised by the Atlas Economic Research Foundation Network, the International Policy Network, the Hanns Seidel Foundation and the Latin American Red Liberal (Liberal Network). In the same spirit, we have helped other think tanks in Latin America to obtain support and contributed to the creation of the Fundación Internacional de la Libertad (FIL), which unites people in Ibero-America and the United States who support ideas similar to ours.

We also train young people who will continue the work of defending and promoting public policies for a free society in the future. LyD organises seminars and workshops for young university students and professionals each year, and awards prizes for the best undergraduate and graduate papers proposing private solutions to public problems. Moreover, we have created a special programme to train young Latin Americans at Libertad y Desarrollo on how to become 'intellectual entrepreneurs', so they can apply their skills after returning to their home countries.

The battle of ideas

It is impossible to describe fully Libertad y Desarrollo's influence on Chilean public policies. Its first achievement was to help prevent the country from turning back the clock on the free market reforms described above and to make contributions towards the country's progress, especially in key areas such as trade and macroeconomic policies. An illustration of that progress can be seen in the Index of Economic Freedom prepared by the Fraser Institute: in 1990 Chile ranked 26th among 113 countries, while by 2005 it had risen to joint 11th among 141 countries. In the case of the Heritage Foundation *Wall Street Journal* Index of Economic Freedom, the country was ranked 14th in 1995, rising to 8th in 2008.

One of our efforts with the most significant results has been the promotion of public policies supporting macroeconomic equilibrium. Achieving low inflation, a balanced budget and a limited state has been an ongoing concern for Libertad y Desarrollo. The fact that the country has reduced annual inflation to 3 per cent in recent years is a source of great satisfaction for the institute.

Another concrete example is our ongoing effort to increase the transparency of the national budget and to monitor and evaluate public spending. Each year, a team of about ten experts is assigned to evaluate public spending proposals and to participate in the debate over the current budget bill. Progress in this area has been enormous, as shown by the increase in Chile's score from 63.0

in 1998 to 87.5 in 2006 in the World Bank's fiscal transparency indicator. (This is the transparency index included in the World Bank's assessment of governance; it ranges from 0 to 100, with a higher value indicating greater transparency.)

Despite these achievements, there have also been tax increases. For example, rates of corporate tax and value added tax have risen. There have been reductions in personal income taxes and tariffs, however. The governing coalition, which is politically centre-left, would like to increase the size of the public sector and the tax burden. Nevertheless, the relative size of the state has remained roughly stable in recent years, at 20.3 per cent of GDP.

Another area of satisfaction for us is trade liberalisation. When Libertad y Desarrollo was founded, Chile's average tariff level stood at approximately 15 per cent. I remember that in one of the first seminars we organised, we proposed that the tariff rate should be reduced to 5 per cent, the average rate among our trading partners at the time. This idea took hold, and the economic authorities acted unilaterally to reduce tariffs: first from 15 per cent to 11 per cent in the early 1990s and later gradually from 11 per cent to 6 per cent by the end of that decade. In addition, the democratic administration decided to seek bilateral free trade agreements with the world's leading economies. Thanks to all of these efforts, we enjoy an average tariff rate today of only 1.6 per cent, thus making Chile one of the world's most open economies. In other words, the view that free trade is an effective tool for progress has prevailed, thus permitting the development of industries that could not have been conceived of 40 years ago. Therefore, the country is now not only a leader in mineral exports, but also in salmon, fruit, wine, forestry products and capital services. Chile is also increasingly becoming an attractive destination for immigrants.

A further high-priority area for our institute has been the promotion of private sector involvement in areas where it was not present before the 1990s. For example, in 1991 we published a book describing the potential benefits of private sector participation in prison services (Libertad y Desarollo, 1993). Studies were also prepared detailing the advantages of private investment in infrastructural services. We actively endorsed the changes implemented by the administration, Congress and the private sector to significantly expand private investment in infrastructure.

Not all of the efforts in the battle of ideas have been successful. Our country has moved backwards in significant areas of our national life, including education. Our proposals to increase freedom in education – to enhance demand-side subsidies to provide parents with greater choice in their children's education, to offer adequate and timely information about the quality of services provided by each school, and to increase the autonomy of individual schools – have not been implemented. Unfortunately, the tendency in recent years has been to limit freedom of choice, increase the Ministry of Education's bureaucratic authority and centralise key decisions on educational issues. Consequently, Chile's achievements have been limited to increases in educational coverage, not in educational quality. In fact, although public spending in this sector has quadrupled, the quality of instruction has remained stagnant. This is especially distressing since the performance of our students at the international level remains poor. Our struggle to move forward in the area of human capital is directly related to this situation.

Labour market regulation is another key area in which our ideas have not prospered as we had hoped. In spite of our efforts, the most influential ideas in recent years have been socialist concepts favouring controls that serve to make the labour market more rigid. This explains why the country's unemployment rate throughout the present decade has been 9.1 per cent, compared with 7.1 per cent between 1990 and 1997.

Nevertheless, we can conclude with satisfaction that Libertad y Desarrollo has played a prominent role in demonstrating that a developing country that bases its public policies on the ideas of a free society can make impressive progress. Today, per capita income in Chile has reached US$13,700 – eight times its level in 1970. Economic growth, job creation and targeted social policies have allowed Chile to reduce the rate of extreme poverty – which affected 45.1 per cent of the population in 1987 – to 13.7 per cent in 2006.

Our experience shows that a think tank promoting the ideas of a free society can achieve success if it has the force of conviction in its ideas and assembles a qualified team of experts. If it can combine solid principles, outstanding technical quality in its research and the ability to exercise influence through wide-ranging networks, its proposals will be taken seriously within the political system. If we add to this the qualities of perseverance and communication skills, I have no doubt that it can achieve a great deal.

Today, however, we must recognise that the battle of ideas can never be conclusively won. I mention this because public policies that lean in the direction of greater state intervention have come to the fore in Chile. Gradual changes have reduced the flexibility of markets, thus limiting the opportunities for entrepreneurship among individuals to flourish. This has reduced the dynamism of the country's economic development. In fact, while the growth rate averaged 7.4 per cent between 1985 and 1995, it managed only 4.2 per cent in the ten years from 1996 to 2006. As a nation aspiring to become a fully developed country, our performance in recent years has been disappointing. It is clear that the battle of ideas is never over and that the responsibilities of Libertad y Desarrollo will be even greater in the future. The challenges of a globalised world – and of the knowledge revolution – will demand even more from us. Consequently, we are determined to continue our active engagement in the marketplace of ideas and public policies with the independence and rigour demanded by this challenge.

References

Blundell, J. (2004), *En el combate de las ideas no se puede tomar atajos*, Caracas: CEDICE.

Büchi, H. (1993), *La transformación económica de Chile: del estatismo a la libertad económica*, Santa Fé de Bogotá, Colombia: Editorial Norma.

Couyoumdjian, J. P. (2008), 'Hiring a foreign expert', forthcoming in S. J. Peart and D. M. Levy (eds), *The Street Porter and the Philosopher: Conversations on Analytical Egalitarianism*, Ann Arbor: University of Michigan Press.

De Castro, S. (1992), *El Ladrillo*, Santiago, Chile: Estudios Públicos.

Larroulet, C. (1993), *Private Solutions to Public Problems*, Santiago, Chile: Libertad y Desarrollo.

Larroulet, C. (2003), 'Políticas públicas para el desarrollo', *Estudios Públicos*, 91.

Libertad y Desarrollo (1993), *Modernización del sistema carcelario: colaboración del sector privado*, Santiago, Chile: Libertad y Desarrollo, Paz Ciudadana Foundation.

Meller, P. and F. Larrain (1991), 'The Socialist-populist Chilean experience: 1970–1973', in R. Dornbusch and S. Edwards (eds), *Macroeconomic of Populism in Latin America*, Chicago: National Bureau of Economic Research/University of Chicago Press, pp. 175–222.

Rosende, F. (2007), *La Escuela de Chicago: una mirada histórica a 50 años del Convenio Chicago-Católica*, Santiago, Chile: Ediciones Universidad Católica de Chile.

Tironi, E. (2002), *El cambio está aquí*, Santiago, Chile: La Tercera-Mondadori.

6 UNIVERSITY FRANCISCO MARROQUÍN: A MODEL FOR WINNING LIBERTY

Giancarlo Ibárgüen S., University Francisco Marroquín (Guatemala)

The work of UFM – because it has been faithful to its mission over the decades – generates a point of reference in the ideological landscape of Guatemala, like a great river or mountain range, something everyone has to take into account, whether they like it or not.

CARLOS SABINO (1944–89),
GUATEMALA, LA HISTORIA SILENCIADA

'Rebellious improvisers'

In 1958, on the eve of Castro's takeover of Cuba, that one of Latin America's first classical liberal think tanks was born. It evolved out of discussions involving a Guatemalan businessman, Manuel 'Muso' Ayau, and a cluster of friends who were concerned about the poverty of their country and what to do about it. At their modest think tank, the Centre for Economic and Social Studies (CEES), they set about studying, writing pamphlets and translating the texts of great classical liberal thinkers into Spanish and mailing them to anyone in Latin America who might or should be interested. The words in these pamphlets echoed throughout Latin America. Peruvian Enrique Ghersi tells us that it was a pamphlet by Ayau in the 1970s, *Ten Lessons for Underdevelopment*, that 'awakened in me the vocation and commitment to defend liberty'. Enrique went on to co-author, with Hernando de Soto, the landmark book *The Other Path*.

CEES was also active in bringing renowned economists to Guatemala to defend the philosophy of freedom and make a case for economic liberty. These visitors included: Henry Hazlitt (1964), Ludwig von Mises (1964), Friedrich Hayek (1965), Leonard Read (1965) and Ludwig Erhard (1968).

CEES pamphlets consistently challenged socialist and Keynesian economic theory and explained the relationship between capital, wages and employment. They questioned the policy of full employment and its impact on salary levels. These pamphlets made the causes and effects of inflation clear and they opposed currency manipulation, import substitution, price controls, minimum wages and agrarian reform. They championed the relationship between free trade and economic growth and the role of the entrepreneur and property rights. Aged thirteen, already an avid reader of the CEES publications that my father received, I sought out Ayau as a mentor. As with Ghersi, he awakened in me a desire to defend liberty.

The decision to found the Universidad Francisco Marroquín (UFM) in 1971 was in direct response to the increasing influence of socialism in academia. The success of the Fabian Society convinced members of CEES that the education of the influential elite was the most important determining factor in the destiny of a country. When they undertook this courageous enterprise, they did so in an environment that was intellectually hostile, politically dangerous and which called for personal risk and sacrifice. Guatemala was the foremost territory for Marxism in Latin America and the first communist experiment – long before Cuba. In the international communist movement, Guatemala was *the* place to be

(Che Guevara was active in Guatemala before going to Cuba). The movement took root in the national university and from there it spread to the private universities. When UFM was founded, guerrilla activity was at its most aggressive.

When Ayau and his supporters – 'rebellious improvisers', as they called themselves – established UFM, they did what few persons have ever accomplished or even dared to attempt. They developed a new model for promoting classical liberal ideas in the world. Ayau applied his great entrepreneurial spirit and creativity to designing an institution that has evolved into something far more significant than an imprint of the man, and with a projection far beyond his country or lifetime.

Entrepreneurship in ideas

Rigoberto Juárez-Paz developed a foundational document for UFM, *Philosophy/Ideario*, which is based on classical liberal philosophy and encompasses all aspects of the institutional structure – its organisation, administration, teaching activities and relationship to society. Although we are a non-profit institution, we run the university as a for-profit entrepreneurial venture in that we subject our own decisions and activities, and those of our staff, to the law of supply and demand.

Flying in the face of traditional academia, UFM does not offer tenure, our board members are business people and entrepreneurs, and our department chairs are required to balance their budgets. In order for us to fulfil our social role as educators, the university does not engage in the political and social issues of the day; rather it focuses on essential themes that transcend contemporary issues. We believe UFM to be globally unique for another reason: we teach all students, regardless of academic discipline (we offer degrees in architecture, business administration, dentistry, economics, education, law, medicine, political and social sciences, psychology and public accounting), the causes and origins of the wealth of nations.

Four core semester-long courses form part of the curriculum for all of the undergraduate degree programmes and these four courses are compressed into two for the graduate-level programmes. Two of the courses, which take a look at economic processes, begin with an analysis of comparative advantage as a fundamental component of the development of human society. The curriculum also covers competition and entrepreneurship, price formation, the role of private property, money and banking, inflation, credit and interest rates, the role of government and the costs of government intervention. The other two courses look at liberty as a philosophical concept. One is based on Friedrich Hayek's *The Constitution of Liberty* and its analyses of the evolution of the concepts of liberty, the rule of law, the use of knowledge in society and the creative power of the free society. The other course contains readings from Ludwig von Mises' *Human Action* and *Liberalism*, focuses on Austrian economics and the influence of philosophy in the history of economic thought, and provides a critical analysis of socialism. Undergraduate students are required to take a fifth course which educates them through a process of analysing real day-to-day issues using the knowledge and tools they have gained in the core courses.

UFM highlights

As civilized human beings, we are inheritors, neither of an inquiry about ourselves and the world, nor of an accumulating body of

*information, but of a conversation begun in the primeval forest and
extended and made more articulate in the course of centuries ...
Education, properly speaking, is an initiation ... in which we acquire
the intellectual and moral habits appropriate to conversation.*

MICHAEL OAKESHOTT

Reaching the best and the brightest

When we recruit students, we look for the most brilliant minds
from all walks of life and those most likely to become future leaders.
Unfortunately, despite our deferred tuition programme, many
cannot afford to study at UFM. The majority of Guatemalans are
very poor, so staying in school and out of the workforce long enough
to graduate from high school is already a sacrifice most families
cannot afford. In 1996 we established the programme known as
ITA (*Impulso al Talento Académico*/Promoting Academic Talent)
to identify the most qualified, passionate, motivated and poorest
students. As well as full tuition, the programme covers room and
board, public transportation, books and basic personal expenses.

ITA students have fire in their bellies – they establish goals
and fight to achieve them. Despite the huge gap in education level,
ITA students quickly rise to the top of the class and actively drive
discussions with their questions. Most of them go on to participate
in graduate programmes abroad and all of them are committed
to changing their country and making sure others do not have to
endure the poverty they have experienced.

Creating a culture of independent thought

In 2003, we began an in-house revolution. We began shifting the

83

focus of what happens in the classroom from *teaching* to *learning* through the intensive use of Socratic practice. We are moving from a culture of command and control, where the professor is the centre of the student's experience, to a more dynamic model whereby the students are actively engaged in facilitating their own learning. This model allows students, under the leadership of their professor, to learn to take responsibility for their learning process and ownership of their curriculum.

Student-centred classrooms facilitate an environment of complex social interactions and behavioural rules which create a culture of intellectual independence, innovation, discovery and genuine learning. We believe that the Socratic method is the best way for students to explore the meaning of liberty. The Hayekian and market process analogies to learning and school culture are numerous and will not be lost on our students.

Challenging the myths

David Hume points out in his essay *Of the First Principles of Government* that when all is said and done, it is public opinion that establishes the limits to liberty. The greatest threats to liberty have been historical myths. Even those that may seem far fetched frequently contribute to the formation of present-day public opinion. For example, the socialist myth is responsible for the death of over a hundred million of our fellow human beings and for the poverty and low living standards of hundreds of millions more. With this in mind, in 2006 UFM established the programme *Explorations on History*, to promote the continuing re-examination of history. We consider this programme *vital* to the future of liberty, in the most literal sense of the word.

Focus on liberty in Latin America

In 2004, the Liberty Fund in Indianapolis selected UFM as a co-sponsor of the programme *Exploraciones sobre la Libertad* (Explorations on Liberty), a Spanish-language version of the Liberty Fund colloquia which is directed towards native Spanish speakers. Held in Guatemala, this programme is targeted primarily, though not exclusively, at a Latin American audience. The programme falls on fertile soil; much has been accomplished in the past four decades to cultivate classical liberal thought in Latin America. UFM's long-standing network of scholars and opinion-makers throughout Latin America is reaching new and stimulating intellectual communities, providing a rich source of networking for participants.

Multiplier effects

The importance of UFM's programmes is palpable in Guatemala. Members of the UFM 'family' have gone on to found a policy think tank, three public policy pressure groups and the first public choice centre in Latin America. Their newspaper columns appear daily in the Guatemalan press and they dominate the influential sphere of talk radio. UFM graduates have mastered the art of taking an abstract idea and putting it into simple language that is culturally relevant and understood by all. Any public debate must take into account a well-documented classical liberal point of view.

Unfortunately, in countries like Guatemala opportunities to change the entrenched and twisted institutional base are fleeting. Luckily, windows of political opportunity do open up and offer us the chance to extend individual liberty by ratcheting down the

85

role of the state as it relates to a particular policy measure or even constitutional reform. UFM has fostered a critical mass of classical liberal thinkers who span several generations and professions. Each has the intellectual ability to recognise opportunities and the courage to honour their convictions and seize them.

Mission possible

The mission of Universidad Francisco Marroquín is to teach and disseminate the ethical, legal and economic principles of a society of free and responsible persons.

Members of the classical liberal community formed by UFM have been directly responsible for the reforms that have had a huge and tangible impact on individual liberty in Guatemala. Sometimes they have participated in reforms as outsiders, sometimes from key positions on the inside. To spotlight the most successful: in 1989 Guatemala's central bank abandoned fixed exchange rates; in 1993 a constitutional reform prohibited the central bank from lending to the government; in 1996 Guatemala's Congress passed the most liberal telecommunications law in the world; and in 2001 legislation was changed to allow competing currencies – an idea advocated by Hayek! As a result of these reforms we have monetary stability, the ability to make contracts in any currency, and phones widely available for everyone. The impact of each of these systemic changes has been so positive that no politicians dare talk of removing them.

The case of telecoms reform in Guatemala is a perfect illustration of the importance of UFM graduates being ready to engage in policy battles. The government nationalised telecommunications in 1971 and by the 1980s setting up a phone line took years and cost thousands of dollars. Just getting a dial tone could take up to fifteen minutes. In response to this, messages and invitations were shuttled on motorbikes around town. The poor and rural areas were cut off from all phone communication. Manuel Ayau fought the state monopoly from its inception. The factor that made the most difference in fighting this battle was the team of UFM graduates who were operating from the inside. In 1995, with a UFM graduate sitting on the congressional committee on tele-communications, a legislative plan to introduce competition into the telecoms market was hatched. The door opened further when the new president appointed him head of the state telephone monopoly. This resulted in very liberal telecommunications laws which successfully privatised phone companies. In 2007, Guate-mala boasted 9 million cellular lines for a population of 13 million and some of the cheapest rates in the world.

As I write, it is election season in Guatemala. An international political adviser recently commented to one of the candidates that he was trying to figure out why there was no talk from any of the candidates or in the media about raising taxes, agrarian reform or other populist formulas. What, he asked, had happened in Guate-mala to make it so different from the rest of Latin America?

Just the beginning

The telephone liberalisation coincided with the arrival of the Internet. UFM was the first campus to be fully wireless and we continue to aggressively use technology to enhance the learning process. Our New Media department provides audio and video streaming of lectures to clients around the world. Both in-house and visiting speakers have been featured, the latter including

Israel Kirzner, Vernon Smith and José Maria Aznar. In addition, the department hosts the Spanish version of Milton and Rose Friedman's *Free to Choose* series and is currently working on a project to fully digitise the entire collection of our Ludwig von Mises Library. The possibilities for the dissemination of ideas of liberty are unlimited!

The founding of UFM was inspired by the example of others who were already engaged in promoting classical liberal ideas. It was the encouragement of scholars, promoters of ideas and friends at organisations such as the Foundation for Economic Education, the Mont Pèlerin Society and Liberty Fund that convinced the founders of UFM to take up the daunting challenge of founding a classical liberal university in a poor country where the battle of ideas had moved beyond rhetoric and into the realm of violence. Today, UFM is a unique and durable venture in the world of ideas; one that transcends Guatemala's borders. UFM has evolved into a model that can be emulated. We believe that UFM can inspire others around the world to undertake and succeed at great enterprises that will continue to expand human liberty everywhere.

> *We take with us the challenge of leading a revolution that will change the course of history in our country. But not with arms, threats or violence; not from ideological trenches that lead us to see enemies in our own brothers and sisters. Rather through open and frank dialogue, through respectful questioning and through the triumph of ideas.*
>
> EDWIN XOL, *MAGNA CUM LAUDE*,
> ITA SCHOLARSHIP RECIPIENT,
> COMMENCEMENT ADDRESS, 2007

7 AWAKENING A SLUMBERING ELEPHANT: CCS IN INDIA

Parth J. Shah, Centre for Civil Society (India)

On my arrival in India in August 1997, after more than ten years of graduate studies and teaching economics in the United States, I resolved to be as self-sufficient in running my new Indian home as I was at manning my American apartment. Cleaning the bathroom and dusting the furniture were indeed more demanding here. When I spent more than half a day paying my first telephone bill, however, and several hours on the electricity bill, my resolve vanished into thin air. I felt utterly helpless; I hired a helper. The dehumanising effects of government monopolies (telecoms and electricity) were no longer a theoretical speculation in the classroom.

But how did I manage to get a house and a telephone to begin with? Rent control and tenancy laws make it nearly impossible to lease any space without close personal contacts. Proprietors not only receive (legal) rents below market rates, but are also in constant danger of losing the property to their tenants. I was fortunate in finding a well-wisher with an apartment with a telephone and gas for cooking. Yes, cooking gas is also a government monopoly. Economically rational laws and the sanctity of contracts were no longer mantras to be recited at classical liberal gatherings.

Widespread abuse of political power, close ties between politicians and criminals, flagrant violation of even basic human rights, censorship of books, plays, films and works of art vividly demonstrated the government's control over not just the economic but also the social and cultural life of India. After her political independence from an alien state, India awaits her civil independence. It was to signify the necessity of economic, social and cultural freedom from the omnipresent Indian state that the Centre for Civil Society (CCS) was inaugurated on 15 August 1997, the 50th anniversary of India's political independence.

It is important to choose critical dates in the life of the institute with care. I capture here a few more observations and thoughts as I look back at the ten-year journey of CCS; it has indeed been a delightful and rewarding journey. Fortunately for me, I met my wife Mana through this work, and she is an even more uncompromising, enthusiastic and energetic champion of liberalism, pushing me as well as helping me to dream bigger and aim higher. Though I write this as a personal account, Mana and my former and current team members are all integral to and responsible for the achievements of CCS.

Why the Centre for Civil Society? Making a statement through the institute's name

It was clear to me that in India the message of liberty would need to be framed differently to how it is framed in the USA – within the historical and cultural context of India. The USA is rather unique in that being free from the state is generally seen as a virtue and accepted as a desirable situation. With the exception of political freedom, which is primarily practised through ritualised frequent elections, statism is the main theme in India. The 'language of liberty', American style, would be too foreign to India.

Second, in the mid-1990s a philosophical battle began between classical liberals and the statists about who would claim 'civil society'. Central Europeans, who revived the idea of civil society in the second half of the twentieth century, thought of it as the space between the family and the state. You do not choose your family and you must be a citizen of a state (at least as of now), and except for the obligations to the family and the state, everything else in life is voluntary. Voluntary action is the domain of civil society. In these theorists' conception, civil society included not only non-profit entities but also for-profit businesses. It was important that civil society be contrasted with political society, and not with business or capitalism. I decided to do my bit in this battle by choosing the Centre for Civil Society as the name of a classical liberal public policy institute in India.

Even though it was conceptually clear that in India the ideas of liberty would be best captured in the language of civil society and in the principles of subsidiarity and 'livelihood freedom', it took quite some time to articulate that approach clearly and consistently. The role of the state should be subsidiary to the role of the people and the government should do only those things that individuals and associations cannot do for themselves. Within the government, the first charge should be given to the local government, then to the state government, and only those tasks that cannot be done by the local or the state governments should be delegated to the central/federal government. This is the broad message that we tried to capture in various phrases. We oscillated among 'Working for a Freer India', 'Developing Ideas that Better the World', 'The Power of Ideas' and 'Social Change through Public Policy'. There is no doubt an apt byline is critical in marketing and branding an institute.

The road to success: models and modes

Everyone in our business has heard the story of F. A. Hayek and Sir Antony Fisher and the formation of the Institute of Economic Affairs (IEA) in London. Looking at think tanks around the world and my experience at CCS, it is clear that there are several different roads to success. These can be summarised in the following five models:

- *Hayek-Fisher Model*: this focuses on the second-hand dealers in ideas – professors, authors, journalists – and works through the trickling down of ideas. Judges are generally not included but they could be one of the most important transmitters of ideas since their judgements set precedents and change the course of legal reasoning. The main tasks embodied in this model are research, writing and dissemination of ideas. Prime examples of the approach include the IEA (London) and the Cato Institute (Washington, DC). George Mason University's law and economics programme has regularly conducted workshops for sitting judges in the USA.

- *Read-Harper-Rockwell Model*: this goes farther downstream than the Hayek-Fisher Model and focuses on students and young scholars. It bypasses the existing second-hand dealers in ideas by becoming the transmitter of ideas to the next generation. Fellowships, seminars, conferences and publications are the primary tasks. Several US-based think tanks are fine examples of this approach – the Foundation for Economic Education under Leonard Read (Irvington-on-Hudson, New York), the Institute for Humane Studies under F. A. Harper (Arlington, Virginia) and the Ludwig von Mises Institute under Llewellyn Rockwell (Auburn, Alabama). In a few cases, fully fledged universities have been created, such as the Universidad Francisco Marroquín in Guatemala and the University of Asia and the Pacific in the Philippines.

- *Feulner-Bolick-Mellor Model*: this focuses on lobbying policy/ lawmakers directly through policy papers, legislative analyses, individual briefings, policy breakfasts and press meetings. Unlike in the previous models, the success is directly visible, even though one might find it difficult to take credit for the success publicly. People in the specific community, however, know why the bill got changed or how it got passed. The Heritage Foundation in Washington, DC, which was founded by Edwin Feulner, is the grandaddy of this approach and a role model for many state-based think tanks in the United States. Judges are also lawmakers but typically it is illegal to lobby them directly on any specific case. Bringing properly chosen cases to court, however – if possible when the judges are likely to be sympathetic – could be a way to 'lobby' the judiciary. The Institute for Justice founded by Chip Mellor and Clint Bolick, based in Arlington, Virginia, has used this method very effectively and has brought about substantial shifts in the legal environment. The International Policy Network in London actively participates in formal meetings of international organisations such as the World Trade Organization and the World Health Organization to voice liberal positions from within. It brings outside pressure on these organisations through the regular publication of articles by local authors in the international media.
- *Chicago-Eastern European Model*: this approach does not worry about changing the larger intellectual and social climate; it attacks policies directly by securing positions of

power or by advising those who are in power. The 'Chicago Boys' in Latin America are one famous example. The break up of the Soviet Union created many opportunities for policy entrepreneurs to work closely with new governments, which lacked policy ideas and the experience and capacity to execute them. The Lithuanian Free Market Institute is one group that fully exploited such a situation; they not only issued policy ideas but also actually drafted bills and at times guided them through ministries and parliament.

- *The Proletariat Model*: different from the Hayek-Fisher Model, which targets intellectuals, or the Read-Harper-Rockwell Model, which focuses on young scholars; this model works directly with the proletariat. It mobilises large numbers of people and groups directly affected by state policies, such as street vendors, taxi drivers, sex workers and unemployed youth. Their primary objectives are to help these people to organise, to provide meeting places and financial support and to conduct mass rallies and stage media events. The Free Market Foundation of South Africa has had good success with this model.

These five models offer a matrix to understand the work of existing institutes. More importantly, they can help guide new think tank entrepreneurs in determining the focus that would be most effective in their country.

The focus of a new institute could also be determined by a different approach – one that considers the type of activities or mode of actions undertaken by the institute. I can identify five basic activities: research, advocacy, campaigns, pilots and poli-cymaking/writing. Research (along with writing and education) could be original or applied; this focus goes well with the Hayek-Fisher Model. Advocacy is not just passive dissemination but, rather, it takes the message actively, regularly and consistently to a target audience that generally includes politicians and policymakers, but could also consist of students, young scholars, lawyers, judges and non-governmental organisation (NGO) activists. Campaigning involves bringing together a large number of affected citizens on a given issue and building a grassroots pressure group to implement change. Pilot projects take the policy idea a step farther by running actual experimental projects to demonstrate the feasibility of the idea and to generate statistical evidence in its favour. The last approach, policymaking, refers to drafting and implementing policy reforms by positioning oneself close to those in power. This could include building capacity within the government to undertake these tasks. The think tank's influence would come from the training and guidance provided to key people in a position to achieve change. The power centre is generally the executive or the legislative branch of the government, but it could be the judiciary. Public interest litigations (PILs) in many Commonwealth countries utilise the judiciary for policy and institutional reforms.

One can imagine a single policy issue going through any of these five modes or different issues playing out in one or more modes depending on the ideological and policy context in a given country.[1] Over the years, CCS itself has traversed these

---

1   It is easy to see how these five modes or approaches correlate with the five models discussed earlier. It would be useful to put the models and the modes in a table, understand their deeper connections and thereby determine a more effective focus of a new institute. Moreover, a great deal can be learned by taking all the institutes in the Atlas directory and classifying them into these models and modes. One can visualise a multidimensional graph or a matrix that captures the

five approaches. Initially, we did research and advocacy through publications, policy dialogues, policy meetings for Members of Parliament (MPs) and Members of the Legislative Assembly (MLAs), and student seminars and research internships. In recent years, we ran a Livelihood Freedom Campaign, which won a Templeton Freedom Award from the Atlas Economic Research Foundation, and a School Choice Campaign. To demonstrate the power of vouchers in offering school choice to poor parents and thereby helping to improve the quality of education, we are now conducting several voucher pilot projects. We are in the process of filing PILs in the Delhi High Court and the Supreme Court to directly challenge some of the country's educational policies. Over time, CCS has moved from research and advocacy to campaigns and pilots, and now works across several of these modes simultaneously.

The objective for a think tank entrepreneur is to look at these five models and five modes/approaches and identify a more effective and efficient way to engage with the process of social change in a given country or area. It is not necessary to view these as distinct models and modes, which work only one at a time. Given the variety of circumstances in a country and the availability of financial resources and, more importantly, human resources, understanding these models can help to delineate an approach that is best for the entrepreneur and the location. The different modes could help differentiate the many issues of concern into the categories of research, advocacy, campaign, pilot or policy-making based on the overall intellectual climate and the policy options being considered by the government. More technical

approaches and issues undertaken by the global think tank fraternity. I leave this task for some other day.

and abstract issues should be dealt with through research and advocacy (i.e. telecoms policy or insolvency law), while issues like the delicensing of street vendors and the legalisation of sex work are more suitable for campaigns. Very concrete reform ideas could be promoted by developing pilot schemes. A triangulation exercise of issues, models and modes could provide a systematic method of determining the appropriate focus for new institutes or changing the strategy of existing institutes.

Get the letterhead right: first a great liberal Board of Scholars

Before and immediately after the formal launch of CCS, our primary focus was on identifying individuals who were classical liberal in approach, and respected and well known in their areas of expertise. Even though the think tank may be a new concept, there are usually several individuals in various walks of life who sympathise with classical liberal ideas and policies. We brought them together and created a Board of Scholars. Listing the names of these scholars on the letterhead opened many doors, provided credibility, and gave us a solid standing in the public arena. They also became our advocates when engaging with government bodies, the media and donors.

Plan, plan; prepare, prepare

Initially, I wanted to start the think tank soon after I completed my PhD at Auburn University. I visited India in the late 1980s and met a large number of people, but the level of support was lukewarm. I realised that I needed to learn the tools of the think tank trade and, more importantly, save enough money to support my personal expenses for at least three years. It seemed possible to raise some money to support the work of the institute, but almost impossible to get support for myself. In India, only the wealthy are expected to engage in such 'social work', and even the law looks harshly on founders of non-profits who draw a salary from the organisation.

While studying economics at Auburn University, I learned a great deal, first hand, by working at the Mises Institute on the campus. Later, while teaching at the University of Michigan-Dearborn, I was fortunate enough to be able to attend several excellent workshops hosted by the Atlas Economic Research Foundation, and I was inspired by Leonard Liggio and Alex Chafuen. I was also encouraged by the network of like-minded people across the world and by the work of institutes such as the Cato Institute (Washington, DC), the Institute for Humane Studies (Arlington, Virginia), the Foundation for Economic Education (Irvington-on-Hudson, New York), the Heritage Foundation (Washington, DC) and the Mackinac Center for Public Policy (Midland, Michigan). The key person who got me to buy my one-way ticket to India, however, was David Kennedy of the Earhart Foundation when he promised to support the institute during its initial years.

I know that I was lucky. Sometimes the best way to learn to swim is just to dive in. As much as possible, however, one must plan, build relationships and learn the tools of the trade. While a spur-of-the-moment launch of an institute makes for a great story, it is not the best recipe for success.

Focus on the youth: developing our own soldiers for the battle

We realised early on that it was quite difficult to find people to do public policy research and analysis from a classical liberal point of view. I had assumed that, by sheer statistical odds, there must be a few public-policy-oriented classical liberals in a country of a billion people. As we all learn eventually, statistical probabilities do not really work in the think tank arena. With the help of our scholars, we started to organise discussions on topical policy issues to develop human capital and establish our presence in Delhi. In addition, we immediately launched a training seminar for college students called the Liberty & Society Seminar (named after an Institute for Humane Studies programme), a four-day-long residential programme teaching them about classical liberal principles and policies. Along with the seminar, we also run a research internship programme called Researching Reality, which allows students to experience and document the impact of public policies first hand. The indoctrination of the Indian youth, who came from a state-dominated education system, was a mammoth challenge for us. Our youth programmes turned out to be a very effective antidote for many of the participants.

Over fifteen of the young people who participated in these seminars came to work with us full time and were responsible for most of our research and publications. In the process, they also discovered completely new careers for themselves in the fields of public policy and research! We actually thought of starting a one-year graduate programme in public policy since such a programme did not exist in India. We are still looking for someone to head this project! One CCS graduate (we call all those who have attended our student programme CCS graduates) has started his own research institute, the Centre for Public Policy Research, in Cochin, Kerala, a state dominated by Marxists since the 1950s.

Putting a human face on liberalism: choosing issues and strategies

CCS is a unique free market think tank in that it directly champions the causes of street entrepreneurs (vendors and cycle rickshaw-pullers), poor parents who can access only government schools, farmers and tribal peoples. Free market institutes are generally viewed as doing the bidding of corporations and the wealthy. We have consciously chosen issues that clearly demonstrate that the classical liberal approach is beneficial to the poor in urban as well as rural areas. Our 'Livelihood Freedom Campaign' talks about delicensing and deregulating street entrepreneurs and the 'Terracotta Campaign' successfully lobbied for giving forest land to tribal peoples.

The 'Duty to Publish Campaign' emphasised the government's duty to provide information *suo moto* (without citizens having to file specific requests for information), which became Section 4 of the new Right to Information Act. The School Choice Campaign advocates school vouchers to break the monopoly of the government on the education of the poor. The classical liberal approach does more for the poor than probably any other philosophy; we just need to find issues to drive home that message effectively.

Novel and sustainable solutions

One reason why CCS has a strong appeal is because our focus is on solutions. We offer novel and at times even radical answers within the Indian context. Most non-governmental organisations (NGOs) spend their time and energy highlighting and magnifying problems. They hardly ever suggest solutions, and the ones that they do suggest typically deal with symptoms rather than the causes. In this NGO environment CCS stands out as the lone organisation that is really concerned about the actual problem and the people being impacted. We contrast 'direct action' with 'policy action' and consistently show the power of addressing social problems through policy and institutional reforms – 'social change through public policy'.

The Chicago School mantra 'if it matters, then measure it' is the right approach to all issues, new and old. One may be philosophically sceptical of the phrase 'measurement is science', but for all practical policy debates, facts, numbers, case studies, tables and charts matter a great deal. One Indian company has a motto, 'In God we trust, the rest must bring numbers to the table.'

Leading and managing: are you the right person for both?

Like many intellectual entrepreneurs, I am an academic – not just by profession but, more importantly, also by nature. Researching, writing and talking about ideas excites me. This can be turned, though not without effort, into intellectual leadership. An equally important part of a successful think tank is managerial leadership. As with any start-up, the initial years run on adrenalin, but as the institute matures, high-quality management becomes critical for growth. At least after three to five years of existence institution-building must become one of the important concerns of the institute. When looking at the think tank fraternity, it is clear that those institutes that have had a sustained impact have been the ones with a team of two people at the helm. John Blundell has rightly emphasised the synergy between Ralph Harris and Arthur Seldon as a key reason for the success of the Institute of Economic Affairs.

Ultimately, ideas are the business of any think tank and ideas must be part of its team training and management. Reminding the institute's staff about the overall vision of the institute, about applying ideas to current issues and cultivating an attitude of critical inquiry, is crucial for the cohesion, motivation and growth of the team. The belief that 'ideas matter' should become a part of the organisational culture. We have tried different avenues over the years: luncheon discussions about the daily news, 'Coffee with Parth', guest speakers, annual planning workshops, human resources retreats and 'CCS Chintan'. CCS Chintan is an internal forum to engage team members in the philosophy and ideas that define CCS and how to apply those ideas to current issues. There is no one formula, but each member must feel that the power of liberal ideas can improve lives and society.

A larger, long-term vision: India a liberal utopia!

Along with the day-to-day policy work, it is critical to talk about an idealist social vision of the institute's work – particularly in engaging with the youth. We talk about the India of today where there is a long queue of Americans outside the Indian embassy in Chicago to pick up their visas to work in India! We ask ourselves: 'What then do we need to do to achieve that?' and 'What makes a good society? And then, how can we get there?'

For other audiences we predict that India could be the first fully and truly liberal society – a liberal utopia – that has bypassed the welfare state and has progressed from free markets to a genuinely free society. Here the institutions of civil society – for-profit and non-profit – not only produce all goods and services, but also care for the needy. Economic statism is losing its legitimacy, but welfare statism is still very dominant. Despite its perverse social and economic consequences, dismantling the welfare state in the West has proved to be a daunting challenge. Some progress has been made, but it is unlikely that the West would be able to convert its state-dominated welfare system to one governed by charity and voluntarism.

In India, the absence of welfare statism, coupled with continued high economic growth in a democratic political system, offers a unique opportunity to build a liberal utopia. Our approach is designed for this goal: define the right size of political society and rejuvenate civil society. Liberal think tanks typically focus on the former, but it is critical that we also look at how to build systems and institutions so that, as the state withers away, people will have the confidence and civil society will have the breadth and the depth to tackle social problems. Unless people see civil society alternatives working, they will be very reluctant to let the state withdraw.

The nature and extent of state intervention in India have been such that an ordinary Indian has little faith in the capacity of the government to do much good. Indians are very proud of the freedom movement that resulted in political independence from the British, and we talk about a Second Freedom Movement for economic and social independence!

Like many of you reading this, I find it hard to imagine doing anything else in life. It is a wonderful journey and a worthy challenge.

8 AN ISRAELI THINK TANK – ITS CHALLENGES AND DISCONTENTS
Daniel Doron, Israel Center for Social and Economic Progress (Israel)

Israel is threatened with extinction and has suffered incessantly from war and terrorism since its founding in 1948. Therefore, it is not surprising that Israelis are almost completely consumed by concerns about security and its political ramifications, to the point of exclusion of many other serious challenges facing them, not least of which are economic ones.

It was in the wake of the 1973 Yom Kippur War, when Israel first suffered defeat, that Israelis finally lost faith in their governing institutions ruled by the Labour Socialist camp. They started asking why their economic system, which boasted some of the most talented people in the world, was lame. For the first time since the country was founded an opportunity to change Israel's economic system materialised.

After the 1973 war, my friends and I – who made up the first generation of graduates from after Israel's independence – developed a deep conviction that we could no longer ignore the countless failures of our entrenched political system and its sprawling bureaucracies. Up until 1973, we tolerated gross inequities and inefficiencies as long as our government assured our survival. It had become clear, however, that the rot in our political system was undermining even our defence establishment. It was posing a threat to our existence and, in the long run, was almost as deadly as the threats from a hostile Arab world.

A handful of us were disgusted by politics and we naively assumed we could bring change from outside of politics. We organised a group called 'The Movement for Change'. We were convinced that the key to reform was to change Israel's strict proportional representation system. This system, we believed, was the chief cause of the political 'factions' which James Madison, a Founding Father of the United States, identified as the chief threats to popular democracy. Factions and the politics of distribution led to ever intensifying struggles over political spoils and generated waste and inefficiency which plagued government services from healthcare and education to justice.

While raising funds for our fledging movement we were rejected by many industrialists and merchants who sympathised with our cause but said they could not alienate a government they depended on in so many ways (subsidies, special tax concessions, permits, land zoning, etc.). This made us realise the intimate connection between political and economic freedom. I had the good fortune to meet notable thinkers, such as Professor Irving Kristol, Arthur Seldon and Milton Friedman, and they deepened my conviction that Israel's political, social and economic problems were rooted in its socialist-statist system.

In the late seventies, I launched the Israel Center for Social and Economic Progress (ICSEP). Its mission: to help Israel realise its enormous potential by freeing its economy from the shackles of a regressive socialist and statist system.

In Israel, economic growth and liberalisation are the keys to survival: only growth will enable Israel to address its many social problems, encourage its young to stay at home and meet its defence needs while striving for peace. It is only through growth that Israel can integrate the massive waves of immigration it has absorbed since its founding.

Israel's dysfunctional political and economic system is perpetuated by an iron triangle of a dominant political system and its unaccountable bureaucracies, oligopolistic businesses and militant labour unions. It is supported by a strong leftist ethos and a belief in big government.

While Israel has a number of successful, globally competitive enterprises (predominantly in high-tech), many of the locally oriented industries are monopolies or cartels. These enterprises restrain competition by keeping politicians and government bureaucrats 'satisfied' and maintain peace among labourers by 'feather-bedding' and inflating salaries. As a result, for decades, Israel has suffered from inflated costs, high unemployment, low productivity (half that of American workers) and slow real growth.

Many Israeli workers earn about $1,200 a month, but prices and taxes in Israel are generally higher than in the United States. About one million Israeli workers receive supplemental government assistance and hundreds of thousands of families cannot make ends meet. Almost half of Israel's $70 billion budget and about one third of its GDP are devoted to welfare, yet poverty remains and may even be growing. The economy operates well below its potential.

A competitive business environment would generate lower prices and could reduce the cost of all consumer goods by about one third. This would increase considerably the purchasing power of millions of poor Israelis who are dependent on government supplementary income and enable them to make ends meet. This, in turn, would enable the government to cut welfare costs and taxes. Basic structural reforms will also enable market forces to unleash the tremendous productivity potential of the Israeli worker and entrepreneur (evident in the high-tech sector), thus propelling Israel into the ranks of the world's most prosperous countries. Therefore, economic reform must become a top national priority.

ICSEP has been providing the know-how needed to fashion, implement and support pro-market structural reforms, and the intellectual ammunition to overcome resistance to them. It has achieved notable successes in generating crucial reforms, including the reform in the financial markets which broke a bank duopoly that was as damaging to the Israeli economy as Japanese banking was to Japan's economy. This was all done despite a culture dominated by out-of-date ideas that resisted and retarded reforms and strong political forces which were determined to perpetuate a monopoly-dominated system.

In addition, ICSEP is at the forefront of the struggle to overcome the pro-Marxist education that dominates most of our universities by inspiring Israeli students through pro-market thinking.

In our policy work, we identify crucial areas in which reform is most urgently needed, including land use, housing, small business regulation, demonopolisation, government structure and function, financial markets, the tax system, labour markets, education and healthcare. We conduct research in these areas and hold seminars and conferences to discuss our findings. We then design concrete reform plans and try to mobilise decision-makers and public-opinion-shapers in order to encourage coalitions in support of necessary reform.

In the mid-eighties, ICSEP laid the groundwork for successful anti-inflationary policies and for the 'privatised' immigrant absorption policies that facilitated the successful integration of the great mass of immigrants from the former Soviet Union. A subsequent ICSEP reform plan, 'Essential Conditions for the Renewal of Growth', detailed a number of concrete steps that could have huge effects if implemented. It was presented to the Israeli government under incoming prime minister Binyamin Netanyahu in September 1999 and to the Knesset (Israel's legislature). A follow-up plan, which updated the earlier plans and provided a detailed analysis of the causes of growing budget deficits and how to cut them, was prepared for Prime Minister Ehud Barak. A third plan suggested steps to enhance productivity by correcting grave distortions in the labour market.

We have also initiated several research projects on major issues, some in cooperation with other bodies, such as the International Center of Economic Growth (on political business cycles, published in *Public Choice*, 1992), and the Koret Foundation (on small businesses in Israel).

We have disseminated our research by organising seminars and conferences for decision-makers which have attracted hundreds of policy people and have been widely reported in the media. They have had remarkable effects on public discourse and have resulted in some significant changes.

Since the early 1990s, we have held workshops and courses for over nine thousand young immigrants from the former Soviet Union, helping them integrate into a Western-style economy. In the mid-nineties, at the request of the Ministry of Education, we also held courses for high school economics teachers.

Since 1998, we have been holding classes in economics in several Israeli high schools and have taught over five thousand student participants. To attract students, we produced a series of short films depicting episodes from the students' lives to illustrate economic principles. The courses teach students basic economic concepts and theories and how they affect their daily lives and career prospects, as well as public speaking skills. The classes are in high demand by students and schools, and we will expand as funding permits.

Since 2000, we have conducted university seminars on 'The Free Market and its Critics' in four Israeli universities. These seminars are primers in the theory and practice of market economics and are based on Milton and Rose Friedman's *Free to Choose* and Thomas Sowell's *Basic Economics*. Students participating in these seminars consist mostly of third-year students and occasional doctoral candidates who are on the dean's list from a variety of faculties.

Usually, the only Israeli students who receive instruction in market economics are those majoring in economics, but they tend to study mostly economic techniques, not philosophy. Other university students – especially in law, the social sciences and humanities – are largely ignorant of economics, which impairs their career decisions as well as their ability to analyse government policies and their cost-effectiveness. Even worse, students are brainwashed by the neo-Marxist and postmodernist ideas that dominate the social sciences and therefore they cannot act as enlightened citizens or decision-makers.

Our university seminars are based on a continuous dialogue between lecturers, students, Israeli entrepreneurs and business leaders and public figures such as former finance minister Binyamin Netanyahu, president emeritus of Dixons, Lord Kalms, and Sam Zell of Zell Enterprises. Close to two thousand students have graduated from our university seminars and many more are on waiting lists. These graduates have changed the atmosphere on the university campuses from one of outright hostility to market thinking to one that is curious about and increasingly accepting of classic liberal thought.

Our alumni also participate in promoting free markets ideas in the public arena outside campus. Some have founded a not-for-profit organisation called 'Citizens for True Social Justice' and have undertaken numerous activities to promote economic reforms.

We are now designing an additional course and alumni club to deepen the students' understanding of market economics and provide them with skills for their public promotion.

In 2005, ICSEP launched a website of ideas, 'Kivunim', which features translations from *Commentary*, the *Wall Street Journal*, the *Weekly Standard*, the *City Journal*, the *Hoover Review*, the *National Review*, etc., to expose Israeli readers to a wider range of thinkers and ideas than is available in the mostly one-sided Israeli media. Kivunim also publishes original works by Israeli writers and its audience includes leading public and intellectual figures. In a short period of time it has gained over ten thousand steady visits a month.

Previously, we published a Hebrew-language periodical, *Lihiyot Hofshi* ('To Be Free'), which featured economic commentary, analysis and information on the Israeli economy. We have also published numerous papers in Hebrew, covering topics such as Britain's pioneering privatisation experience, deregulation, the benefits of privatisation for the environment, and the proceedings from our various conferences. There are over twenty titles in circulation. ICSEP has also translated into Hebrew seminal works such as Milton and Rose Friedman's *Free to Choose* and

James D. Gwartney and Richard L. Stroup's *What Everyone Should Know about Economics and Prosperity*; adapting the latter to Israeli circumstances.

Currently we are preparing a book about the recent historic financial market reforms initiated by Finance Minister Binyamin Netanyahu in cooperation with ICSEP and other public bodies. This was the first time that a reform was launched in Israel with collaboration between government and voluntary bodies – providing a valuable lesson for Israelis who doubt that change can be made under the present political circumstances.

ICSEP has been bringing leading personalities to Israel to share their knowledge and experiences. Our distinguished guests have included: Nobel laureate Professor Milton Friedman, Professor Irving Kristol, Ambassador Stuart Eizenstat, US Supreme Court Justice Antonin Scalia, Judge Richard Posner, George Melloan of the *Wall Street Journal*, former UK Commissioner for the Common Market Sir Leon Brittan, and prominent businessmen such as Samuel Zell, Lord (David) Young and Lord (Stanley) Kalms. We are also regularly consulted about the Israeli economy by foreign study missions, such as the US–Israel Joint Economic Development Group and the US Congressional and White House study missions, as well as by foreign journalists and television networks and economic think tanks from Europe and the United States. ICSEP has also acted as a source of economic expertise for many other institutions, including the Israel Chambers of Commerce, universities, the Israel Supreme Court's Institute for Judicial Studies, the Israel Management Institute and others.

ICSEP has enjoyed extensive media coverage of its activities. Thanks to ICSEP's sponsorship, Israeli television has twice broadcast Milton Friedman's *Free to Choose* with Hebrew subtitles, a special on the difficulties of free markets in Israel and a film on immigrant entrepreneurship. Ironically, ICSEP's director, Daniel Doron, was a member of the Government Central Planning Board, on which he preached against central planning, and he also served on Prime Minister Netanyahu's Economic Advisory Group. He has appeared on international television and has been quoted on the topic of Israel's economy by *Business Week*, the *New York Times* and *Forbes* magazine. He regularly writes for the *Wall Street Journal*, the *Weekly Standard*, the *Sun*, and occasionally for the *Financial Times* and the *National Review*. Doron is also regularly interviewed on Israeli TV and radio and has published extensively in the Hebrew press. In addition, ICSEP's board members regularly publish articles, make media appearances and participate in public commissions on topics such as tax reform, housing and monopolies. These activities help to give ICSEP's ideas increased exposure.

ICSEP has focused its work on educating and engaging with the policymaking community. It has reached legislators, senior government officials, jurists, the media and academics, as well as leading figures in industry, labour and commerce. ICSEP has supplied them with the information necessary to pursue growth-oriented reforms.

ICSEP has transformed the terms of the economic policy debate in Israel. When it began its work, the concept of 'market economics' was unknown, ignored or derided. Today, public opinion has changed dramatically. Israeli policymakers do not wrestle with the question of whether Israel should reduce government interference in the economy; they consider exactly how, where and at what speed it should be reduced and how to overcome resistance to change. Each of ICSEP's conferences and seminars has attracted extensive media coverage along with participants from the highest echelons of the Israeli policy community: presidents, Supreme Court justices, government ministers, Knesset members and other leaders from a variety of fields. ICSEP was also the winner of two Atlas-sponsored Templeton prizes – one in 2005 for Institutional Excellence and the other in 2006 for Student Outreach. ICSEP's work has served as a significant catalyst for initiating reforms in various sectors of the Israeli economy.

It is precisely because Israel had such a statist economy that it presented great reform opportunities. We have learned a lot from experiences in other countries, but when it comes down to it, all reform proposals had to be modified to suit the specific nature of Israeli institutional structures. We also learned to take advantage of political opportunities, although much work remains to be done.

As for our integration in international efforts, it is a pity that despite the good work done by Atlas to create a network of pro-market think tanks, the achievements of these organisations do not come close to those of market adversaries, statists and collectivists. We must all strive to do more to devise new strategies and achieve better results.

9 IBL: BRINGING THE MARKET BACK TO ITALY

Alberto Mingardi, Istituto Bruno Leoni (Italy)

Italy is not best known for its free market economists, but it would be ungenerous to say that the country lacks a tradition of classical liberalism. During the nineteenth and twentieth centuries, Italy was home to quite an active group of *liberisti*; that is, intellectuals who had a proper understanding of the virtues of the free market and who added considerably to the global capital of scholars versed in the ideas of liberty. Two figures that come to mind are Vilfredo Pareto and Gaetano Mosca. But it should not be forgotten that the school of '*scienza delle finanze*' exercised a decisive influence on James M. Buchanan and on the development of public choice theory. The extensive network of friends and admirers of Luigi Einaudi (president of Italy, 1948–55) shows the prestige that this important scholar garnered within the economic profession and beyond.

Nevertheless, despite their authoritative scholarship, these intellectuals have exercised a limited influence in the shaping of Italy's economic policies over the last century. The mastermind behind Italy's unification, Camillo Cavour, was by and large a free trader, and Marco Minghetti, a banker and one of Italy's first prime ministers, had a deep grasp of classical liberalism. The whole of Italy's political class from the beginning served the special interests of a few, however, and backed a policy agenda imbued with protectionism, industrial policy, compulsory welfarism and, eventually, war, which blossomed with the rise of fascism.

In the aftermath of World War II, the transition from monarchical to republican rule and from authoritarianism to universal franchise democracy left Italy's economic policy largely unchanged. While Mont Pèlerin Society member, and friend of Ludwig von Mises, Luigi Einaudi was the governor of the Bank of Italy and the head of state, his popularity and ability to secure appointments was based on his fame and honesty, not on his classical liberal ideas.

As in many other countries, during the sixties and seventies the intellectual debate in Italy was completely monopolised by the academic left. Keynesianism was widely accepted as the only sensible approach to economic matters, and we were so good at producing socialist economists that we ended up exporting them, a prime example being Piero Sraffa. Only a small number of individuals had the courage to speak of the importance of private property rights, the free market and limited government. Bruno Leoni was the foremost Italian classical liberal scholar of the second half of the twentieth century, but he died tragically in 1967 at the young age of 54. In the years after Leoni's death, Sergio Ricossa was the only prominent Italian economist to preach consistently the gospel of classical liberalism. Alas, he was almost entirely alone; on the left as well as the right.

I do not intend to bother the reader with a pedestrian sketch of contemporary Italian history, but we are today a product of our past. Ideas, both good and bad, have consequences. The dominance of statism in Italy can help explain why general government revenues were 24.8 per cent of GDP in 1960, 36.9 per cent in 1980, 42.4 per cent in 1990 and 47.9 per cent in 1997. It also explains why the number of Italy's government employees increased from 7.7 per cent of total employment in 1960 to reach 16.2 per cent in 1992, and why general government expenditure has risen dramatically since the late nineteenth century, from 13.7 per cent of GDP to around 30 per cent before World War II, 30.1 per cent in 1960, 42.1 per cent in 1980 and 53.4 per cent in 1990. What we see here are ideas at work. Ideas provided the impetus for an unprecedented growth of the state; a growth that faced very little opposition.

Italy was not lacking intellectual ammunition against statism, but the absence of intermediaries cultivating new 'second-hand dealers' in classical liberal ideas was certainly evident. The only attempt to create a classical liberal think tank in Italy dates back to the mid-1980s, when Antonio Martino, who had an extensive network of acquaintances both in academia and in the think tanks of the Anglo-Saxon world, founded the Centro Ricerche Economiche Applicate (CREA) in Rome. Martino, who headed the think tank, became the president of the Mont Pèlerin Society and later the minister of foreign affairs in 1994 and the minister of defence in 2001–06. Virgilio Floriani, a successful entrepreneur with a firm belief in philanthropy who backed Martino's think tank, admired the success of the Institute of Economic Affairs and the willingness of his friend, Antony Fisher, to export that model all over the world.

CREA published the works of James M. Buchanan, Milton Friedman, Henri Lepage, Alvin Rabushka, Gordon Tullock and Roland Vaubel, along with those of well-known Italians such as CREA's Antonio Martino, Sergio Ricossa, Franco Romani and a giant of political science, Gianfranco Miglio. Under Martino's leadership, CREA was responsible for introducing concepts such as the flat tax and school vouchers into the Italian debate.

Unfortunately, CREA did not last long. Floriani, despite his business connections, was unable to raise enough money to sustain his brainchild. Italy does not have a tradition of philanthropy and an independent think tank is inconceivable in a country where the state is almost the only donor. Moreover, at that time the political parties dominated the entire political scene. Little was discussed outside of them and they engaged only minimally with others within civil society.

Something was about to change, however. At the end of the eighties, the scale of corruption – knowledge of which had been confined to a few political circles – became apparent to the general public. The vast expansion of the state, particularly in the south, was the method by which the political class relentlessly bought votes for itself. While it was not a revolution yet, crisis was in the air and the judiciary targeted part of the political system and jailed its main actors. The former Communist Party was a major benefi-ciary. Nonetheless, owing to overwhelming dissatisfaction with the old politics, the left was not able to secure power during the 1994 elections and the Italians voted in a complex coalition that included newcomers such as Umberto Bossi's Northern League and Silvio Berlusconi's Forza Italia.

While both of these parties ended up being disappointments to free market advocates in Italy, they did succeed in using free market rhetoric when fishing for votes. For example, Forza Italia's 1994 platform advocated a transition towards a flat tax. In the eighties this idea was unheard of and now it was entering the political debate through the front door.

Alas, right-wingers have been poor allies of good policies. In 1994, they stayed in office for too short a time to be judged, and when they were in office during the second Berlusconi government from 2001 to 2006, little was accomplished. Although Berlusconi's government was successful in achieving a partial relaxation of hiring and firing regulations (though not on the firing side), on the whole its libertarian-leaning rhetoric went no farther than the paper it was written on.

At the same time, during the nineties, the Italian state was rolled back. The main drivers in this process were not the 'freedom fighters' who joined the political right, but the technocrats who, for the most part, stayed with the left. In particular, the director general of the Italian treasury (now the governor of the central bank), Mario Draghi, was a key player in the privatisation process. With left-of-centre governments, Italy had an impressive array of privatisations, including highways, telecommunications and electricity. It can be argued that the process reflected the need to reduce public debt rather than an ideological affection for private enterprise. Regardless, Italians saw the light with privatisation.

This is just one sign of how the world changed profoundly in only a decade. The end of the Soviet empire and the subsequent emergence of globalisation rearranged the vocabulary of politics and the communist left had to start shopping for new ideas. Free markets, long considered a problem, now looked increasingly like the solution. The consensus in the economics profession began to change, and even though economists were by no means predominantly libertarians, they were no longer Sraffians either.

Thus it comes as no surprise that classical liberal ideas were reinvigorated in Italy. The nineties brought a re-emergence of a free market movement that had not been seen since the early 1900s. Much of the credit for this reawakening is given to three small publishers: Aldo Canovari (Liberilibri), Leonardo Facco (Leonardo Facco Editore) and Florindo Rubbettino (Rubbettino

Editore). These publishers empowered a new wave of enthusiastic free marketeers who wanted to translate into their native language the classics of liberty ranging from F. A. Hayek to Murray Rothbard. The printing presses rolled and Italian readers had access to Murray Rothbard's *The Ethics of Liberty*, David Friedman's *The Machinery of Freedom*, Frederic Bastiat's *The Law*, and many others. Thanks to the enthusiasm of Professor Raimondo Cubeddu, Bruno Leoni's masterpiece, *Freedom and the Law*, was translated into Italian for the first time 35 years after its publication in the United States. The number of advocates of classical liberalism in academia and in journalism multiplied as well. The Internet proved to be the perfect mechanism to connect the few libertarians in different cities who thought that they were alone in their thinking.

Italy didn't have a free market think tank until late 2003, when the Istituto Bruno Leoni (IBL) was founded. Istituto Bruno Leoni was developed, in part, as a result of disillusionment with the Berlusconi government, which, instead of walking the road towards a free market, embraced the flag of protectionism. IBL also intended to foster a greater 'institutionalisation' of the free market activities that had taken place in previous years. IBL was founded by three young scholars, Carlo Lottieri, Carlo Stagnaro and myself, with the support of three businessmen. The idea of starting such a venture was stimulated by a variety of factors. Personally, I had spent a few weeks in 1999 as a summer intern at the Heritage Foundation, Washington, DC, and was fascinated by the extent to which think tanks are intellectual powerhouses in the United States. Moreover, I had the great fortune of being under the benevolent wing of Lord (Ralph) Harris of High Cross, and I was increasingly fascinated by his intellect as well as his charm, ethics and fierce commitment. I began to see his career and life as a model to follow; despite the fact that it would be impossible to be as good as him. My colleague, Carlo Lottieri, was convinced that there needed to be an umbrella institution to help younger scholars to pursue classical liberal research within Italy's academia, which was an inhospitable environment dominated by socialists of various kinds. Seeing the Centre for New Europe established in Brussels and other think tanks starting up in Europe gave us the courage to found IBL.

But unintended consequences are always more important than planned ones. I have found that thus far IBL has been responding to three basic outcomes which none of us could have conceived of accomplishing, but which exceeded our expectations.

The first is the extent to which the base of our movement is not defined by numbers, but rather by human types. Fund-raising forces us to present our ideas in a bourgeois, 'presentable' fashion. It is not just a matter of attracting the money that interested individuals may want to spend on research, and the people interested in undertaking such research, it is about getting an intellectual movement more actively integrated into the real world. We can even say that part of our job is to educate our donors; not just about the research projects IBL is trying to develop, but also, at least initially, about the kinds of philanthropic efforts that lie behind a think tank.

The second outcome is that we started engaging in public policy. This was, and still is, a novelty in Italy. There is something to be said for the fact that there is almost no accurate translation of the word 'policy' in Italian. Right from the beginning IBL started publishing policy papers. By doing so it was competing with other actors that traditionally have proposed legislation – the trade unions and business associations. They, of course, have far more gunpowder than a small free market think tank. Nevertheless, it is important that we have succeeded in bringing our ideas into the marketplace as well, potentially providing the political class with the inspiration necessary to bring about change. This has not been an easy task. We have had to persevere and find a proper balance between the radicalism of our ideas and the practical policy recommendations derived from them. We wanted to keep open windows of opportunity, even for small, incremental reforms, without watering down our fundamental principles.

We have published a Briefing Paper every single month since our inception; which now adds up to 55. These papers are distributed to over fifteen thousand people, including all the Italian Members of Parliament. Over the course of three years, we have published 53 Occasional Papers (papers with a more theoretical and general touch), over a hundred 'Focuses' (shorter papers tailored to Internet readers) and over thirty books. Our website now has more than nine thousand pages and over a thousand visitors a day, which is not bad for a website written exclusively in Italian. Far more important, the authors of our papers range from very established figures, such as Nobel Prize-winner Ed Phelps, world-famous novelists like Mario Vargas Llosa and prestigious social scientists like Anthony de Jasay, Israel Kirzner and Vito Tanzi, to a number of committed young scholars, most of whom were not around when IBL was founded or were 'converted' to our ideas later on. While it is not easy, we do our best to find an appropriate balance between works with long-term objectives (in which IBL promotes fully fledged libertarian ideas) and policy-oriented publications, whose tone has to be different because their 'consumers' are directly involved in politics.

The third beneficial consequence of founding a think tank was that we reached a level of public visibility that was unthinkable without one. Being well organised is still the key to becoming known, and IBL's consistency in its work has given it the reputation of being the flagship of the type of policies that it pursues. The increase in the quantity and quality of our output has helped us to gain a reputation with the press. Moreover, our ideological consistency has resulted in us being viewed as extremists on some issues, but also as intellectually honest and therefore trustworthy. We tend to have dialogue with our enemies more often than fights. Italy is the country of Machiavelli and people can sense when you are selling out. Honesty has therefore been the best policy for us.

These three outcomes epitomise the 'intellectual entrepreneurship' behind the daily work of our think tank. Working in an organisation whose survival is dependent upon its capacity to raise money to grow, and whose capacity to raise money depends (at least in part) on its output, we are forced to think differently and dynamically. A fair proportion of our time is devoted to developing ways to improve our communication and of taking advantage of all the possibilities that come with an Internet-based society. In addition, a fair amount of time is devoted to increasing our customer base by reaching out to politicians, journalists and other groups that can be convinced of the benefits of free competition.

A think tank can be seen as a vaccine against the tendency towards self-marginalisation that is often typical of fringe intellectual movements. We are already beginning to see the fruits of our labour blossom.

To say that IBL has had a significant impact on policymaking would be self-indulgent. While we are making inroads, a major, truly revolutionary reform has not yet been accomplished. Nevertheless, we see the Italian public discussion evolving, day after day, in a better, more informed, more market-oriented direction, and our role in that process is not negligible. It is not the end, and it is not even the beginning of the end, but rather, merely the beginning.

10 OPENING TAXPAYERS' EYES: AN UPHILL BATTLE AGAINST TAXATION IN JAPAN
Masaru Uchiyama, Japanese for Tax Reform (Japan)

Margaret Thatcher, Britain's prime minister from 1979 to 1990, was heavily influenced by the thinking of Friedrich von Hayek. Hayek believed that economic prosperity could be achieved through a reduction in taxes, deregulation, a sound financial system and a decrease in government expenditure. In addition to Hayek, Sir Antony Fisher, who founded the Institute of Economic Affairs (UK) and the Atlas Economic Research Foundation (USA), was also a powerful catalyst for her achievements. I am profoundly grateful to the Institute of Economic Affairs for providing an institutional model for the Japanese for Tax Reform (JTR) – a foundation and grassroots organisation that promotes lower taxes in Japan.

Historical reasons for Japan's high tax burden

The growth in the size of Japan's government has its origins in Japan's democratisation process. In accordance with the advice of Rudolf von Gneist of Berlin, Hirobumi Ito (Japan's first prime minister in 1885) established the Imperial Constitution in a way that prevented Congress from meddling in three areas: diplomacy, defence and the economy. Through this constitution, the Emperor became a 'demigod' and the elite bureaucrats working for the 'god' improved their standing. *Dajyokan*, the top bureaucrats, were able to obtain significant consular power. In 1945, the Emperor declared himself 'human' because of defeat in World War II. From this point on, bureaucratic organisation became the responsibility of the person who held the highest position of authority within the government. Since the enlargement of bureaucratic growth and waste cannot be stopped, the tax burden keeps growing. The bureaucrats are also employed as board members of big companies, enabling the government to control the Japanese market. The current nominal national tax burden is 40 per cent of GDP, but the actual tax burden is much larger and is estimated to be over 60 per cent of GDP. Moreover, there are discrepancies between the government-issued data and independent studies, so the precise percentage is unknown.

Libertarian ideas as a solution to high taxes in Japan

In September 1996, I organised a lecture for Grover Norquist, the president of Americans for Tax Reform (ATR). His simple message, which was rooted in libertarianism, resonated with me. A year later, while working as the chief operating officer of a small-to-medium-sized company in Gyoda City, in Saitama Prefecture, I established JTR as a vehicle for bringing those ideas to Japan as a way of addressing our large tax burden. Exactly seven years after founding JTR, I resigned from my job and dedicated myself exclusively to serving as the president of Japanese for Tax Reform. Using my retirement allowance for operating funds, I opened an office in Akasaka, Tokyo. JTR, an independent organisation that does not receive any support from the government, believes in lower, simpler and fairer taxes. JTR considers this combination essential to Japan's economic revitalisation, along with a limited role for the government in the economy and the promotion of economic freedoms. This is the basis of the tax-reduction movement that JTR has started. The JTR movement is a collaboration of think tanks, grassroots coalitions and educational institutions. JTR believes that the formulation of a social network to support these groups is extremely important.

Challenges to liberalism in Japan

Since I founded JTR in 1997, trends in the private sector, academia, the non-profit community, the media, parliament and education have been anything but supportive of liberalism. In the private sector, many large companies and members of the Federation of Economic Organisations are controlled by the central government and employ high-level government officials. In exchange for agreeing to the requests of bureaucrats, these companies receive benefits from bloated government coffers, which inflate the prices of commodities for taxpayers.

Since high-level government officials are now being criticised for accepting jobs within the private sector, they are flocking to academic positions at universities in Japan. There are numerous 'bureaucrats-turned-professors' in Japanese universities, and these institutions are becoming increasingly dependent on government subsidies. This trend has led to an exponential increase in the number of academics known as '*Goyo Gakusha*' (government scholars), who try to maintain and enlarge the vested interests of the government. Only '*Goyo Gakusha*' wield authoritarian powers and receive financial compensation as members of government consultative bodies and committees.

Of over twenty thousand non-profit organisations which

currently exist in Japan, 95 per cent receive funds and subsidies from the government and almost all non-profit organisations are under government control and subject to irrational taxation systems. There are many organisations that call themselves think tanks, but almost all of these think tanks are controlled by Kasumigaseki (the Japanese Central Government). Kasumigaseki controls them by providing their subsidies and human resources – there is little genuine competition.

The Ministry of Internal Affairs and Communications has the right to give approvals and issue licences for broadcasting and reporters have to report exactly what the government announces. Moreover, the structure of bureaucratic organisations centred on Kasumigaseki diffuses into local administrative bodies. The nature of the Japanese taxation system makes local government revenues fragile. Local governments cannot operate without payouts from central government. They have very little financial autonomy and central government makes most of the decisions regarding the allocation of resources. In addition to the harmful effects of such a centralisation of power, allowing government the freedom to exercise policy discretion creates economic paralysis.

Japan has a parliamentary system that consists of 480 members in the House of Representatives and 242 members in the House of Councillors. Ninety per cent of the bills proposed are government sponsored and lawmaker-initiated legislation is rare. Moreover, approximately 16 per cent of Diet lawmakers were previously administrative officers. Lawmakers preach 'small government' to taxpayers; only a few, however, sign our Taxpayers' Protection Pledge (see below). In short, they align themselves with 'big government', which continues to increase taxes.

Compulsory education is conducted by teachers who are

members of Nikkyoso – a communist trade union. While they make elementary schoolchildren learn calligraphy, composition writing and slogans, children are also indoctrinated with the idea that 'paying taxes is compulsory and that taxes make society better'.

JTR has been involved in a number of activities designed to address this situation. The following section briefly describes the most important of our initiatives before detailing the success of our Taxpayers' Protection Pledge.

Spreading the message
Tax Freedom Day

Tax Freedom Day is the first day of the year in which a nation as a whole has theoretically earned enough income to fund its annual tax burden. In 2008, we calculated this day to be 27 May. In addition, we also calculate the number of working days needed to generate enough tax revenues to pay for government expenditures and call it 'the day to think about the government expenditure'. In 2008, this day was 8 June. We post both of these days on our home page and in *JTR News*.

Educational lectures

We deliver speeches across Japan on Tax Freedom Day and throughout the year on the merits of lower taxes and smaller government. We believe that a transaction should start from the offer of 'Give me what I want, and I will give you what you want'. When both parties are satisfied with the trade, they say 'thank you'. Good trade makes people happy and can cross several borders: private, local and national. Nobody says 'thank you', however, when you pay tax. The wealth of the nation should be measured by the number of times people say 'thank you' rather than GDP. We also conduct quizzes and questionnaires via the Internet on these topics, and we are receiving a lot of feedback supporting our position of smaller government.

Weekly 'Wednesday meeting'

Beginning on 3 March 2004, we have held a meeting every Wednesday at JTR's offices for people who want to be free from political interference. We discuss the problems of big government and appropriate responses. These gatherings were inspired by the weekly meetings of Americans for Tax Reform.

Monthly strategy sessions with Diet members

In addition to our Wednesday meetings, every month we work with the Leadership Institute Japan and the Institute of Public Accounting to sponsor 'strategy sessions' for Diet members of both chambers at the Diet Members Hall. Unfortunately, we have had to suspend the strategy sessions for the time being owing to an anonymous document we received that contained defamatory statements about our activities and questioned our use of public facilities.

International meetings and partnerships

In July 2005, through the network of the Atlas Economic Research Foundation, we developed connections with think tanks and social entrepreneurs in a variety of countries. These connections helped to facilitate our membership of the World Taxpayers' Association and other networks. In 2007, we were awarded a Templeton Freedom Award grant from the Atlas Economic Research Foundation and gave a presentation on coalition-building at State Policy Network's Pacific-Rim Policy Conference in May 2007.

The Taxpayers' Protection Pledge

One of our most important activities is the Taxpayers' Protection Pledge. We ask incumbent lawmakers and candidates to sign a pledge that opposes any tax increases. They are also expected to maintain balanced budgets. In any democratic country, taxes are borne by taxpayers with the consent of an electoral majority. Budget deficits, however, result in a greater financial burden for future generations – children who may not have had the opportunity to consent to those taxes will be charged. No Japanese central or local governments can sustain budgets that supersede the tax revenue for more than forty years. Unfortunately, the policy whereby taxpayers have a choice in taxes is now gone. The purpose of this pledge is to ensure that lawmakers promise voters 'small government' and that they advocate specific policies that support that objective. Once a year, on Japan's Tax Freedom Day, we publish a newsletter, *JTR News*, which is distributed to pledge-signers, interested individuals and potential donors. In 2007, we distributed 3,200 copies of *JTR News*.

The public accounting system developed by the Institute of Public Sector Accounting run by Dr Hiroshi Yoshida was crucial to this pledge process. This system helps pledge-signers to see the connection between the management of public finance and the tax burden on future generations and helps to identify the right person for making decisions about taxes. JTR asks pledge-signers to prepare an accounting statement in accordance with the accounting principles outlined by the Institute of Public Sector Accounting and the Taxpayers' Protection Pledge. The Institute's system prepares two balance sheets: the taxpayer's balance sheet and the governor's balance sheet. The public goods being provided are recorded in the taxpayer's balance sheet. The payment commitment by the governor is recorded in the liabilities of the governor's balance sheet and the source of the payment and other assets are recorded in the assets section of the governor's balance sheet. The difference between the assets and the liabilities in this balance sheet represents the future tax that will be charged to Japanese citizens.

Fukuma case study

The town of Fukuma in the Fukuoka Prefecture employed this system in 2002. In 1999, when the local government started the system, a taxpayer's future tax was 56,000 yen ($US467: based on an exchange rate of 120 yen to the US dollar). By 2005, it had become negative by 64,000 yen ($US533) as the budget had moved from deficit into surplus.

This proves that a capable person can maintain balanced finances. It also shows that if decisions about taxation and tax disbursement are the responsibility of an incapable person, then taxes will be utilised poorly. The Institute of Public Sector Accounting's system strives to explain this to the person in charge of taxes and encourages him to orient his daily activities in such a way that when determining taxation and tax disbursement, he strives for a balanced budget. This is analogous to the way a business manager expects an accountant to focus his daily activities on improving the company's profitability.

While JTR asks candidates who sign the Taxpayers' Protection Pledge to oppose any tax increases, this does not necessarily mean that all lawmakers have the ability to keep the pledge. This shows how valuable this accounting process is in providing accountability for pledge-signers by recording tax decisions.

Effective policies are liable to meet with high resistance

Despite the effectiveness of this strategy in achieving JTR's goal of lower taxes, it has been met with high resistance. For example, on 10 December 2003, when asked by Tetsuya Kobayashi, a member of the prefectural assembly, about the proposal to introduce the Institute's accounting system, Kiyoshi Ueda, the governor of Saitama Prefecture, spoke favourably. Unfortunately, while this proposal would help to protect the assets of residents of the prefecture from bureaucrats who were planning to introduce new taxes, it has yet to be introduced into the assembly.

In 2005, the mayor of Ushiku City in Ibaraki Prefecture stopped employing this accounting system owing to 'political judgement', even though it had been recommended by a civic organisation (loosely connected with JTR). Between 2006 and 2007, a pledge-signer, Chozo Nakagawa, mayor of Kasai City in Hyogo Prefecture, decided to employ the accounting system, but, for unrelated reasons, a no-confidence motion was submitted against him and the assembly was disbanded. Fortunately, he gained the confidence of the citizens and was re-elected. At the extraordinary session of the assembly after re-election, a budget was initially allocated before a no-confidence motion. After the session, Mayor Nakagawa learned from the section manager of finance that no budget was allocated for public accounting and that it was intentionally deleted by staff in the finance office. Despite this, Mayor Nakagawa continued to promote the system, saying: 'As an autonomous body in financial difficulties, it is more important for us to implement it ahead of other autonomous bodies by employing stringent standards that exceed those of the Ministry of Internal Affairs and Communications.'

These instances serve as evidence that useful policies are liable to be met with high resistance. Originally, this law was designed to protect the liberty of an individual from oppressive rules and restrictions by persons holding political power.

The good news

In addition to these activities, I was instrumental in persuading a publisher to produce a Japanese translation of *Human Action* by Ludwig von Mises, from the Liberty Fund version. It will be published prior to the Mont Pèlerin Society meeting in Tokyo in September 2008. The Japanese translation has been out of print for many years. Professor Toshio Murata, who was a student under Mises at New York University in 1959–60, and who initially translated *Human Action* into Japanese, continues to fight for his beliefs despite old age. He is a great role model and has had a tremendous amount of influence on us.

The government's control over taxes takes away people's freedom. This should not be forgiven and should be minimised. We will continue to fight to promote this agenda and make sure taxes are simpler and lower across Japan.

11 A SHORT STORY OF THE FREE MARKET: BETWEEN THE TWO UNIONS
Elena Leontjeva, Lithuanian Free Market Institute (Lithuania)

When I was a child, I never saw bubblegum, only a wrapper, which somebody brought to school for our amusement. Yet I learned from an empty wrapper that the bubblegum must exist. In the same way I discovered there must be the market, even though there was no market in my environment. 'Market', the word itself, sounded sinful. No wonder! This was a time when socialism was being 'developed' and embraced as never before. Naturally, we did not know about such things as free choice, supply and demand, bubblegum and bananas. The content of a sweet-smelling bubblegum wrapper was beyond my wildest imagination when I was eleven, but when I was sixteen that all changed. My dream came true and I started working at a newly launched bubblegum production facility, the second one in the USSR. It looked as if the socialist state could catch up with the market.

While working at the conveyor belt, however, I witnessed striking social injustice and economic inconsistency, which led me to the question: what changes must be made to make the system work and prevent people from being pushed to one single solution – stealing from their workplaces? For a while I studied mathematical programming, economics and industrial planning, hoping that this would be the way to improve the system. Unfortunately, my work as a programmer did not make the country any better and made me feel disillusioned. I remember the day back in 1986 when I realised that socialism must be improved by way of market forces and I started to contemplate how exactly the market would alter the system. I was still expecting to reconcile the market with socialism, however, and it took me several years of personal perestroika to comprehend that the market implies private property and that the system will not be saved by increasing the 'independence' and 'self-finance' of state enterprises.

In 1990, Lithuania declared independence and thus broke the Soviet empire. Freedom of speech and movement allowed people like me to bring ideas into action. For five young econo-mists led by Professor Glaveckas, this meant establishing a think tank which we called without compromise the Lithuanian Free Market Institute (LFMI). There was no doubt in our minds that it was time to contribute to building a new order; one based on indi-vidual liberty and limited government. Many scholars and profes-sionals joined us, excited by the idea of building a new Lithuania. I dropped out of postgraduate studies without regret and ventured into the newly established institute. We were privileged with only a month or two of academic serenity to sketch out the free market principles before life provided a chance for us to jump into the reform-making process.

A new law on commercial banking came under consideration in parliament, and since we knew that a well-functioning market starts with capital allocation, we outlined a proposal on banking principles in Lithuania. Even though we were young and inex-perienced, our proposal competed on an equal footing with the official draft of the central bank and even won the sympathies of the members of the Economic Committee of the parliament. This was the start of our success, but also of continuous hardship. The central bank became our long-term opponent and made our lives truly difficult. At one point, our one-room office was taken away, but we persevered and continued to contemplate the future of banking while sitting in entrance halls and other unsuitable places. One of these places was a conference hall in the central bank, which we dared to use since it was always empty and had a table and chairs on the stage. Looking back, the situation seems rather ironic: the system attempted to push us out of the arena and, in response, we climbed on to the stage.

The allergic reaction of some statesmen towards us was understandable; we were a new 'beast' in public life: a non-profit private institution which instructed authorities how to run the country. We did not wish to be arrogant, but our mission required us to visualise where and how to move forward, to enlighten people and to steer those in power in the right direction. In addition, we vowed that we would not accept government funds, a principle that we followed strictly. This made the authorities worry: we had a state-level agenda, but no state affiliation. Yet, at that time, private funds were seldom available. As a result, our finances were uncomplicated and recorded in a thin notebook. This notebook did not reflect the most crucial donation: our efforts, which were donated for free to the free market cause. This was the key investment which formed the foundation of the Institute.

Despite all the difficulties that we faced during the early years of our think tank, it was a very precious time. There was no alternative to freedom in people's souls and minds. Free trade and private property had no bona fide alternative. To be able to provide people with bread, not to mention sausages and bananas, former socialist states had no other solution but the free market. Some countries realised this right away and others not until much later. Lithuania was the first in the former USSR to liberalise prices and started mass privatisation, around the same time as the Czechs.

Lithuanians enjoyed the most freedom when the reforms were being commenced. Old socialist rules and regulations did not have moral support among the rulers or the general public. Almost instantaneously people could trade without restrictions, do business without regulations, cross borders without customs and create wealth without paying excessive tax. This was the time when most of the initial capital in Lithuania was being created and, more importantly, when people were learning principles that they were never taught in their socialist schools. Responding to the needs of the day, we developed the legal framework for, and contributed to the founding of, the first Lithuanian commodities market. This gave people a platform on which to exchange goods at a time when there was a shortage of almost all goods and, more importantly, buyers and sellers did not have a mechanism for interacting with one another.

The next issue that needed addressing emerged from mass privatisation: almost all people became shareholders of former state companies, but they had no rights in the companies and no mechanism for trading their shares. Our response to this problem was to develop a set of legal principles for the capital market and the stock exchange. This not only allowed the trading of shares and bonds on the market, but also made it possible to raise capital and define shareholders' rights. As a result of theses efforts, the first stock exchange in the former USSR was opened in Lithuania in 1993. The development of the Securities and Exchange Commission followed.

In our work to develop a system of institutions, our aim was to provide the impetus for the adoption of a minimum set of rules to protect private property, rather than giving way to interventionist regulations. Beginning in 1993, Western countries and donor institutions began to transfer their 'know-how' to our soil, and while they were often our allies in promoting a reform agenda, at other times we had to fight against their efforts to bring about more intervention and rent-seeking behaviour. It is well known that our region suffered from bank bankruptcies in the mid-nineties. The primary reason was that while donors worked hard to introduce capital adequacy and other sophisticated ratios into the banking system, nobody noticed that there was no proper mortgage system, so the same property could be used as collateral multiple times. I recall many more cases where shallow interventionist regulations preceded indispensable rules.

Reflecting back on those times, I regret that we were not able to address all of the pressing issues of the day, yet I know that we always chose the most important ones that would result in a chain reaction. The most vivid example of this is the introduction of the currency board in Lithuania. When Lithuania was getting ready to replace the Soviet rouble with its national currency, litas, we were promoting the idea that money should be separated from the state, although at that time it didn't sound very attractive. But when the new currency was introduced and the central bank launched harsh interventions that led to a remarkable appreciation of the young (or new) national currency, the economy was brought to a standstill. We felt the need to explain to people that it was not the market which made the national currency rise, but the central bank, which is a typical central planning authority. We told people there could be no genuine market if currency remained in the hands of central planners. Since many academic economists and public officials were great enthusiasts of the traditional (interventionist) central bank, it was crucial to show people that there might be an alternative. Only 50 years ago Lithuania enjoyed the gold standard and people still had memories of sound litas, so we appealed to people's hearts and minds, explaining the benefits of gold and other sound money. The currency board model was a kind of a modern version of sound and relatively independent money. Explaining to people its essence, which is very simple, and which was called by opponents the 'lavatory principle', was only the first step. Let me give you the basics as well: the central bank can issue currency only in exchange for foreign reserves and gold, which must be kept in its vaults, and must exchange any amount of national currency at the fixed exchange rate and vice versa. This operating principle means that the hands of the central bank are tied – no credit expansion, no interventions, no relevance.

Sure, very few people shared the vision that turning the central bank into a 'lavatory' could save our freedom. Fortunately, among those few was the prime minister. We kept sending numerous policy papers to statesmen, appealing to people through the media and speaking to the business elite and politicians. Despite widespread scepticism and the hardcore opposition of the central bank, the currency board model was introduced on 1 April 1994 through the Litas Credibility Law. This law tied the national currency, the litas, to the US dollar at a fixed exchange rate and required that all money in circulation be fully backed by gold and foreign reserves. Despite critics' prophesies that the currency board would not survive and that it was on the brink of crashing, thirteen years have passed and the system is still alive. It has survived many crises as well as official political plans to dismantle it. Thanks to the currency board, people's money was never devalued or used to cover bank losses, treasury shortfalls or to finance the grand plans of statesmen. For thirteen years people were protected from central bank interventions and currency fluctuations caused by the central planning authority. Needless to say, the currency board broke down artificial barriers that separated Lithuania from global money and capital markets, and interest rates decreased at a rapid rate that even we found surprising.

After the implementation of the Litas Credibility Law, there was no shortage of local and foreign critics who claimed that a developing economy would not survive without some currency devaluations and that such devaluations would help to promote exports. As the US dollar appreciated (yes, there were such times!) many began panicking and worrying that the devaluation of the litas was imminent. The interest groups lobbying for devaluation were so powerful that it is a miracle that the devaluation never actually happened. These groups were happy to support the euro as the new peg instead of the US dollar, since the euro at that time was steadily weakening. In 2002, this was done as part of national efforts to join the European Union. Unbelievably, from that time onwards the euro started to appreciate! It would be difficult for graph-lovers to counter my guess that the currency which Lithuania chooses as an anchor is always strengthening and that this fact alone is responsible for developments on the Forex market. On a more serious note, our history is proof to devaluation devotees that it is still possible to prosper economically and to have fast-growing exports without this economic 'remedy'.

Since the monetary system was now in order, we turned to other areas of importance. At this time, there was a lot of concern about the country's competitiveness, so we provided comprehensive policy proposals and suggested that officials should focus on addressing the burden of the state: taxation, expenditure and regulation. Our fight on this front has been quite productive: personal income tax was set at a flat rate and remains flat despite many attempts to implement progressive rates. The property tax for individuals that has been on the government agenda for about a decade has never been introduced (except recently for commercial property). The discussions on the corporate profit tax have been varied. At one point, the idea of abolishing the corporate tax became so popular that it was included in the electoral programmes of two competing parties. Reinvested profits have not been taxed, which has helped to boost private sector development. Unfortunately, owing to harmonisation pressure from the European Union, the Lithuanian government did not dare abolish the corporate profit tax and even returned to the old practice of taxing all profits by a universal tariff, which is currently at 15 per cent.

Our efforts to retreat from the pay-as-you-go social insurance system have been partially successful – the transition is set in motion and private pension funds have already become common. Needless to say, more radical steps need to be taken. Working at a think tank requires a lot of patience; there were times back in the 1990s when proposing the introduction of private pension insurance provoked harsh criticism and disbelief that it could ever be implemented. My highly esteemed Chilean friend, José Piñera, said that some people believe that a private pension system succeeded in Chile only because it is a very long and narrow country. If, in less than a decade, private pensions were successfully introduced in petite and heart-shaped Lithuania, tell me, what else is impossible?

What is noteworthy about LFMI is that life gradually required us to engage in an exceedingly wide variety of topics. How can one work on budget issues and not touch upon agriculture? How do you address agriculture and not tackle the most interventionist case: white sugar? These questions led us to get involved in almost every topic associated with economic and social policy. These topics included pensions, social redistribution and welfare, the functions of government and strategic planning, as well as a nationwide initiative on reducing the size of the state, which came to be known as 'sunset'. We launched an assault on business over-regulation, known as 'sunrise', and engaged in the topics of competition policy, market entry and licensing. We introduced the concepts of education reform and vouchers and put forward the idea of the private sector becoming involved in health insurance and provision. The Institute developed solutions for fighting corruption and engaged in issues related to public administration, transportation, the energy sector and the knowledge economy. This is in addition to our own field: NGO regulations, philanthropy and the principles and procedures of law-making.

Although such wide-ranging engagement is common sense and frequently leads to good luck, it is tiring and consuming. People expect us to act on any issue that becomes hot in the public agenda. Journalists call us on matters that go far beyond our expertise.

LFMI is an interesting case since it is a truly genuine domestic initiative which, in the early years, had no helping hand from abroad and almost no access to foreign know-how. It was not until after 1993 that we developed relationships with foreign partners. In addition, being one of the first think tanks in Lithuania also meant that there was no history of non-governmental organisations in the country or a tradition of private funding to support such initiatives, so we were leaders in defining what it meant to be a think tank. We were also pioneers in conducting independent research and advocacy, educating the public, engaging in non-partisan policy efforts and actively fund-raising for our activities. Every skill beyond our initial mission has been developed in response to daily demands, and we have learned to be inventive and very efficient. Our scope and our output always looked suspiciously big vis-à-vis our budget, and I have heard people say that we must employ at least one hundred people. We have become an incubator for countless statesmen and stateswomen, and LFMI staff have been highly desired, and from time to time recruited, as ministers, deputy ministers, state councillors, central bank board members and advisers to the president and prime minister. Early members of the Institute currently hold top positions within private industry as well as finance and public administration. LFMI fellows teach at universities and publish widely in the press. Many of them become 'celebrities', since they frequently appear on television and radio.

It is not yet the right time to rest on laurels, however. Our homeland today is the European Union, and the many similarities between the EU and the Soviet Union make me worry. Lithuania's accession to the EU and the transfer of the ideas of the welfare state from the West pushed us off the free market road on to what must be a 'road to serfdom'. The ideological climate in Lithuania is deteriorating. After years of confidence in spontaneous order, many people started to presume that changes in the market could be foreseen and that instead of waiting until the market brought desired results, authorities could intervene and 'take care' of the changes. The massive transfer of EU subsidies makes our people believe that the 'centre', whatever that is, knows better about where to invest and whom to favour. The economy is being damaged by enormous central support and harmonisation, and it is increasingly difficult to find a genuine market around. All of this is a great misfortune, but we know from our socialist past that bad times are never for ever.

I will admit that it is not easy to address the infinite policy matters and countless institutions of the EU. We feel obliged to speak to people, however, about the vicious omnipotence of the Union and the principles that would make the EU downsize to a sound level. Dealing with this matter from just a utilitarian point of view is fruitless. We need to begin talking to people about faith and the moral foundations of liberty. If people are not ready to accept the spontaneous way of life, then the prospects of freedom are dim. Without a deep acceptance of spontaneity, people will always seek to set up institutions that attempt to provide certainty, which will most likely be institutions of serfdom.

12 FIGHTING FOR ECONOMIC SANITY
Alexander R. Magno, Foundation for Economic Freedom (Philippines)

The Foundation for Economic Freedom

In 1995, an otherwise reformist Filipino government backed down before immense populist pressure. This exemplified the need to establish an institution that advocated free markets.

At that time, the oil industry in the Philippines was heavily regulated and the government decided the price of oil products, which politicised the whole process. In order to avert price fluctuations, the government maintained an Oil Price Stabilization Fund (OPSF), which, in theory, collected oil when world crude prices were lower than pump prices and subsidised pump prices when imported oil was more expensive. In practice, however, the Fund was in constant deficit, required special appropriations to maintain it, and became a mechanism for subsidising oil prices.

The OPSF was one of the major reasons why the government suffered from chronic deficits that forced it to keep borrowing and further aggravated the country's indebtedness. Domestic prices were *always* lower than the price of imported fossil fuels because it was too politically costly to raise oil prices to market levels. For decades, oil prices remained the most provocative political issue, and every time oil prices were raised, transport strikes occurred and militant groups spilled on to the streets.

This sort of regime did not cause any discomfort to the three oil companies that were the only ones allowed to operate in the country at that time. Under the heavily regulated regime, the oil players were guaranteed a fixed return. All the price uncertainties were absorbed by the national coffers and, therefore, by taxpayers (regardless of whether they owned vehicles or not). Car owners enjoyed 50 times the oil subsidy of those who used public transport. The arrangement was patently anti-poor, although public opinion never understood it as such. Conventional opinion held that if prices were allowed to rise, the poor would be harmed because of higher food prices.

Around the middle of 1995, the rising cost of world crude forced the government to increase fuel prices and, as expected, the move was met with massive popular opposition. This opposition was catalysed by militant leftist groups for whom oil price increases were a reliable rallying issue that enabled them to broaden their constituency.

Weeks before mid-term elections were due to be held, a large coalition called Kilusang Rollback (Rollback Movement) took to the streets. The coalition included left-wing organisations, trade unions, student groups, opposition politicians and Catholic bishops. After several large protest demonstrations, the government, anxious about the electoral fallout from enraged public opinion, agreed to roll back oil prices.

The price cut had two effects: increased oil importation that year and billions of pesos in special budgetary allocations to cover the operating deficits of the OPSF. The increased demand for oil indicated that the price was wrong. It encouraged imprudent consumption of an imported product whose unwise use led to adverse environmental and health consequences. Moreover, the public sector deficit widened, the peso weakened and inflation spiked. The domestic economy flagged.

There was another event which illustrated the insanity of conventional economic wisdom at this time. Unwilling to antagonise militant rice farmer groups in an election year, the government postponed the importation of this staple commodity. By the second half of the year, a serious rice shortage occurred, forcing rationing.

Rice is a heavily protected and subsidised crop in the Philippines, as it also is in Japan and Indonesia. In these countries fresh water can be scarce and high energy costs for pumping water from aquifers make the cost of producing crops substantially higher than in the mainland economies of Thailand and Vietnam. The cultivation of rice is part of the country's religion, however, and subsidising its retail price is considered an obligation of government – even if it worsens the budget deficit.

To this day, the Philippines trades tariffs on manufactured products at the World Trade Organization negotiating table in order to maintain its protection for domestic rice producers. This has led to severe distortions in the country's economic development, including the hollowing out of labour-intensive industries and the stagnation of agricultural productivity. By law, only the government can import rice. As the ripple effects of a badly conceived land reform programme take their toll, domestic rice productivity continues to fall and imports continue to rise.

The rollback of reformist policies and its disastrous fiscal consequences compelled a group of academics, retired policymakers and businessmen to hold a series of meetings to discuss the prospects for advancing market-oriented reforms in an environment where populism shapes government responses. As they say, the squeaky wheel gets the grease. In the pseudo-populist democracy that prevails in the Philippines, those who protest the loudest are the ones who shape policies – even if these policies are destructive to the majority over the longer term.

Market reforms in a statist and heavily regulated economy create immediate pain for vested interests within the status quo, while the potential beneficiaries of these reforms benefit farther down the road and thus are probably unaware of the rewards they stand to gain. The trade unions in the heavily protected manufacturing sectors, for instance, know that trade liberalisation will cost them their jobs, but the larger number of unemployed who stand to gain from expanded trade do not know they will be beneficiaries of liberalisation. The unemployed are unorganised and politically insignificant. The same analysis can be applied to rigid labour policies that benefit the minority that is currently employed and limit the economic prospects of the majority that is unemployed.

The dilemma of pro-market reformists is always that their constituencies are unformed – and uninformed. They do not dare to act against vested interests, conventional wisdom or organised economic orthodoxies. The latter are particularly important in the Philippines, where economic autarky is closely intertwined with the mainstream nationalist sensibilities associated with the struggle for independence. This is reinforced by a widely held view of government as a generous provider of subsidies for everything from housing to utilities to agriculture, a view fostered by many decades of government reliance on taxing trade rather than relying on economic expansion to generate revenues. The administration of taxes has historically been weak while tariff protection has been high.

The group reviewing the prospects for reform under such

adverse political conditions decided that an advocacy organisation needed to be formed to improve public economic literacy, take unpopular positions on current public debates, run against the grain of prevailing public orthodoxy and engage in discussions with powerful lobby groups.

The organisation would have to be high profile as well as bare boned. It would be unlikely to receive much support from the oligarchy and at times it could be unpopular with the political class, which is inclined to follow the drift of populist opinion in order to win elections. It would therefore have to rely on the superiority of its argumentation, the quality of its research and the collective credibility of its members. Such an organisation, the Foundation for Economic Freedom (FEF), was born in 1996.

Advocacy

Given the specific circumstances of its formation, FEF's first step was to tackle the economically insane oil industry regime that was in place at the time. The group issued position papers supporting the deregulation of the oil industry. A law reflecting these suggestions was eventually passed and the industry now has about thirty players and is profitable without a peso in subsidy.

Fellows of the Foundation were previously involved in advancing policies that opened up the telecommunications monopoly. Before liberalisation this sector was monopolised by the Philippine Long Distance Telephone Company. Communication costs were high and service was remarkably bad. Liberalisation paved the way for the introduction of state-of-the-art communications technology, which came in at precisely the same time as wireless communications became prevalent.

FEF also supported the comprehensive tax reform package introduced by the Ramos government; specifically, the introduction of the value added tax, which more evenly distributes the weight of taxation to the consumption side. The comprehensive tax reform package, along with the expanded VAT introduced during the presidency of Arroyo, helped correct the fiscal position of government, reduce the propensity to borrow, relieve the once debilitating debt burden, and set the stage for the present-day low-inflation and low-interest-rate regime.

The huge subsidies required to maintain the once nationalised energy sector also contributed significantly to the budget deficit. The National Power Corporation made enormous losses. Paralysed by bureaucracy, it was unable to anticipate the rising demand for power, which led to severe shortages. Moreover, it was not able to make the necessary investments to produce energy more efficiently. This led to some of the highest power bills in the region, crippling the country's ability to build a competitive manufacturing sector and attract industrial investment.

The FEF supported the passage of the Energy Industry Reform Act, a complex piece of legislation which opened the way for the privatisation of government assets and fostered competition through open-access arrangements and the unbundling of the transmission business from power generation. This measure facilitated private investment in the energy sector and the privatisation of generation assets. Privatisation reduced the need for subsidies and created sources of revenue to reduce the budget deficit.

Owing largely to the Retail Trade Act of 1954, which restricted ownership in the retail trade to Filipino nationals, the Philippines had one of the most inefficient retail industries in the world. This resulted in a retail mark-up that was almost triple the global benchmark. This large retail mark-up harmed the poor the most, even though the nationalist defenders of this law claimed to be defending the thousands of small retail corner-store operations that mushroomed in an inefficient economic sector.

The FEF led a campaign to liberalise the retail sector and open it up to investment. In this campaign, the FEF found itself waging a bitter public relations battle with left-wing economic nationalist groups supported by the retail cartel. A retail liberalisation act was eventually passed in 2000. Its benefits are now widely felt in terms of lower mark-ups and greater retail competition, despite restrictive provisions inserted in the law by populist politicians.

The FEF likewise participated in the 'Freedom to Fly Coalition', which campaigned for an open skies policy. This campaign found itself up against a duopoly that kept air transport prices high and service limited. Although still ongoing, the campaign helped ease protectionism in the airline industry and opened the way for a more competitive atmosphere that supports both tourism (which has expanded rapidly in recent years) and cheaper transport of domestic products across the archipelago.

Since 1996, the Foundation has produced scores of position papers, research reports and briefing manuals, covering a wide range of issues from economic policies to the quality of governance and the rule of law. It has sustained a high public profile in all the major policy debates and has played a prominent role in the passage of nearly every key piece of reform legislation over the last decade.

Relying on the profile and record of its Fellows, the Foundation has had an impact disproportionate to the meagre resources it has managed to raise to support its campaigns. FEF is a small organisation, but the collective reputation of its membership has given us tremendous influence in the policy arena – far in excess of our research capacity as an institution. Four of the last five economic planning ministers in the Philippines were members of the Foundation, and the former prime minister, Cesar Virata, chairs FEF's Board of Advisers. Several members of the Ramos, Estrada and Arroyo cabinets, including Ramos's finance secretary, Roberto de Ocampo, have been Fellows at the Foundation and have helped to raise its public profile. The secret here lies in the ability of the Foundation to use the media to broadcast its positions and form alliances with other groups in order to sustain individual campaigns.

A better society

My work with the Foundation for Economic Freedom represents the completion of a long journey from the political left. I was a high school student in the early seventies doing volunteer work in the slums of Manila when I first encountered left-wing politics. I was organising religion classes in the impoverished communities while Maoist militants were organising those same communities for the revolution. In the face of heart-wrenching misery, the salvation I preached seemed distant while the revolution they promised seemed more imminent. In that revolution, the state was the instrument for instant relief for the poor. I was seduced.

That was a period of political ferment: the politics of the country had become highly polarised and events came in quick succession as the crisis deepened. The communist movement grew rapidly in these conditions, drawing support from a broad student movement, organised workers in factories, radicalised farmers' associations and an articulate section of the Catholic clergy.

When military rule was imposed in 1972 and a brutal dictatorship gained power, political options quickly narrowed. The mainstream political parties simply evaporated in the face of repression. The underground communist movement became the rallying point for all anti-dictatorship forces. Arrest, torture and imprisonment did not diminish my inclination for radical politics. Repression steeled my determination to fight the tyranny, even if it meant allying with the communists. The political conditions pre-empted all other choices and cancelled all grey areas in thought as well as action.

Involvement in left-wing politics, however, raised more questions than the pervasive orthodoxy could manage to answer. I spent the early part of my adult life as an academic and public intellectual specialising in Marxist structuralism, but as I strove to master the literature, it became more and more evident that the conceptual standpoint had no explanatory value. It could not explain the economic and political realities of the day.

All currents of the Filipino left draw heavily on the imagery and discourse of the anti-colonial struggles waged against Spain and the United States. They romanticise economic autarky and fear trade linkages with the West. Uninformed by modern economics, these perspectives romanticise nationalisation and state control of assets. They promise redistribution but have no notion of wealth creation. This antiquated paradigm relies on the heavy hand of government to determine market behaviour and consequently restricts political and personal freedom. It is therefore inherently anti-libertarian in every dimension of social life.

The popular uprising of 1986 was a historical as well as a personal turning point. The political left completely failed to anticipate the overthrow of the dictatorship. What they had contemptuously dismissed as the 'middle forces' – democrats and entrepreneurs – determined the turn of events, provided a workable vision of where our society should go, and laid down the democratic ethics on which modern governance ought to be built.

The political left had long been an ideological and organisational relic from nineteenth-century thought. That became evident after democracy was restored and government policy became a matter of public debate. At almost every point of policy contention, the left represented the reactionary, anti-progress position.

My work as an advocate for a free economy in a free society over the past two decades has consistently pitted me against my former comrades in the left-wing groups. The public debates served to sharpen the concepts by which people could make free choices on policies that shape our lives. They demonstrated, at every instance, the superiority of free market choices in bringing our society closer to the vision of economic and political freedom.

Our economy has progressed significantly since democracy was restored. We have achieved fiscal stability, strengthened investor confidence and created a dynamic and competitive national economy. These improvements would not have been possible if our public had remained embedded in the old statist, inward-looking and merely redistributive paradigm that once held their imagination captive.

13 THE WAR OF IDEAS: THOUGHTS FROM SOUTH AFRICA

Leon Louw, Free Market Foundation of Southern Africa (South Africa)

The course of events is a Hayekian 'spontaneous order'. Accordingly, its determinants are complex and obscure. A great diversity of people, institutions and interests try to influence the course of events, and invest substantial resources to do so.

Since the net effect of all this effort, ingenuity and wealth determines the fortunes of individuals, organisations, countries, regions, cultures, religions and life on earth itself, it is surprising how little scholarly analysis there has been on how best to influence outcomes. What there is tends to be in political science. Scatterings exist in sociology and psychology. As one of the referees for this chapter put it, 'some of the so-called "think tanks" are disguises for certain individuals whose goal is not a better future for their country but rather that their photographs appear in the newspapers ... they certainly show that in fact they could not care less about the principles of freedom (or, for that matter, principles of any sort)'.

For those of us who believe that one of the most decisive determinants of events is economic policy, there is virtually nothing on the subject in economic science. Policy analysts and 'activists' have sessions at conferences on 'strategy' which usually entail reports on what people are doing rather than analysis of what works.

In the first edition of *Waging the War of Ideas*, lifelong strategist and doyen of classical liberalism John Blundell made a unique and pioneering contribution to the subject – essential reading for anyone wanting to make a difference. My contribution to this edition has no pretensions of being scholarship. I have been asked for personal conclusions drawn from practical experience over forty years in the ideological trenches of South Africa's transition from apartheid, and my not insignificant experience in other countries combined with my modest role in the global war of ideas.

A crucial insight from our South African experience is that people fortunate enough to be doing the right thing in the right place at the right time often have decisive impacts. While there can never be certainty about causality, there are compelling reasons to believe that our work before, during and immediately after the transition in South Africa made a substantial contribution for the better. Curiously, convincing though the evidence might be, our role and even our presence are scarcely reflected in literature about this period.

The first decisive role we played was in masterminding the economic policies of one of South Africa's historically black homelands, Ciskei. We were invited into that role as part of a philanthropic contribution by the Anglo-American conglomerate towards 'development' in the region. They offered our services to the homeland government. The long story cut short is that we went to great lengths to secure support from the then banned anti-apartheid movement, and ended up formulating detailed policies that transformed the area into a free market enclave with predictably spectacular benefits. It became the only 'homeland' to increase revenue from internal sources, despite the fact that most forms of revenue were abolished or reduced substantially. There was, for instance, zero income tax on companies, apart from a 15 per cent withholding tax (on profits repatriated from the area).

Personal income tax was reduced to a flat rate of 15 per cent, starting at a threshold so high that 90 per cent of taxpayers ceased paying any tax at all. A multiplicity of other revenue sources, such as land tax, stamp duties, licensing fees and many more, were entirely abolished. The government was persuaded to implement this when we showed that the combined government–private cost of collection was nearly as high as the revenue itself, and more in some cases. Over eight hundred statutes were repealed and small businesses were exempted from most forms of regulation.

Apart from experiencing spectacular economic growth, Ciskei became South Africa's only homeland with an 'influx' problem ('white' South Africa maintained 'influx controls' to curtail the flow of black South Africans from other impoverished 'home-lands' to 'white' South Africa).

Our second decisive, and historically much more significant, role was our influence on South Africa's transition from apartheid. We encouraged the apartheid regime to liberalise and privatise during its twilight years by divesting itself of much of its property and regulatory power before abdicating. Then we encouraged negotiating parties to adopt sufficient 'checks and balances' in the new constitution to protect people out of power sufficiently to ensure that they would submit peacefully to those in power. Finally, we encouraged the new government to replace its former socialist policies with pro-market policies that improved South Africa's score significantly on 'freedom', 'economic freedom' and 'competitiveness' indices. Predictably, the new 'left-wing' government was accused by the left of betraying the revolution and selling out to neoliberals.

It is seldom possible to say whether similar results would have occurred without the work of pro-market activism, but the coincidence in matters of detail between what we were propagating and what happened makes it probable that our role was decisive. The constitution, for instance, has provisions which, as far as we know, were uniquely propagated by us, and which are not found in other constitutions.

Lamentably, our courts have virtually interpreted our constitution out of existence. From this we learn at least two important lessons: first, the critical importance of precise unambiguous terminology, and second, that key actors need to operate within and fully comprehend the significance of a properly informed climate of opinion generated conterminously with the rule of law.

The following section summarises the general lessons that can be learned from our local and international experience.

Aerial bombardment versus trench warfare

Participation in the war of ideas falls into two broad categories: that which is aimed at influencing the climate of opinion ('aerial bombardment'), and that which is intended to influence individual policies ('trench warfare'). The first great pioneer and exemplar of classical liberal aerial bombardment was the Institute of Economic Affairs (IEA) in London. Aerial bombardment entails influencing the climate of opinion within which policymakers work, primarily by way of research and publications. It is premised on the assumption that policies are a reflection of what policymakers regard as politically expedient for the time being, rather than objective evaluation of the evidence. If policies were the outcome of weighing the evidence objectively, there would be much greater international consensus.

Policymakers are, in truth, followers not leaders – they see where the crowd is going, get in front and say, 'Follow me.'

Aerial bombardment is, by its nature, a long-term strategy. It entails influencing society's intellectuals – academia, media, civil society, authors, consultants and advisers.

The climate of opinion was so thoroughly influenced in a classical liberal direction that it was presumed by many, most notably Francis Fukuyama, to have been entrenched permanently as the prevailing paradigm at 'the end of history'. It seems increasingly clear, however, that the price of freedom is indeed eternal vigilance, that there is no end of ideological history, and that power reasserts itself against liberty eternally, changing substantially in form, but never in substance.

There are no irreversible situations or 'laws' of history of the kind popularised as mistaken and dangerous old Marxist recipes. The outcomes in human affairs will always depend on what we are capable of doing every day. Paradoxically, communists and socialists who beat the drum of 'historical determinism' never thought they could leave history to roll in on the wheels of inevitability. Socialists in general work more diligently at influencing history than the supposed defenders of freedom. They take more seriously the dictum 'put your money where your mouth is', which is the main reason why most institutions that work to protect individual rights and property rights are insufficiently funded.

Two of the most ominous manifestations of dirigisme in new clothes are policies being popularised and adopted as the supposedly appropriate responses to both climate change and the 'war on terrorism'. Liberty is presently experiencing a profound setback, which is in sharp contrast with post-cold-war euphoria, when classical liberal activists seriously considered organising an international 'victory celebration'. Their premature optimism is reminiscent of communist intellectuals proclaiming 'Victory is at hand!' during the 1970s.

I met an ageing classical liberal journalist, Robin Friedland, recently, not having read anything he'd written or seen him for 25 years. He said he was writing a book on what he regarded as the most important issue of modern times: climate change. 'Let me guess,' I said, 'you're sceptical about it.' Indeed he was – as are almost all people who favour human liberty.

Why are classical liberals so predictably sceptical? Is there a distinctive classical liberal climatology? Of course not. Their scepticism, and the equally predictable blind faith in the opposite direction of dirigistes, is not really about climate change, but about the fact that it has become the new weapon with which enemies of liberty subvert private property rights and legitimise a more invasive state through the amplification of collective control, which is the inevitable result of subjecting property to the 'tragedy of the commons'.

The second great issue, the war-on-terrorism erosion of civil liberties, entails a perplexing conundrum: the erosion of civil liberties to 'protect' citizens from the terrorist threat to civil liberties. Enemies in war become unwitting allies against freedom. Benjamin Franklin observed in 1759 that 'Any society that would give up a little liberty to gain a little security will deserve neither and lose both'.

The trench warfare approach tends to characterise activists and institutes in developing countries, leading examples being Hernando de Soto's Institute for Liberty and Democracy in Peru, India's Liberty Institute, and the Free Market Foundation in South Africa. Trench warfare entails such 'practical' and 'pragmatic' activities as submissions to government in response to published policy proposals, meetings, workshops, articles and media appearances – all dealing with a specific public discourse about an imminently proposed reform.

Developing countries have two distinctive features. First, they seldom have mature or even clearly identifiable climates of *intellectual* opinion. A greater proportion of policy development appears to be a direct ad hoc response to whoever happens, for the time being, to have the dominant influence, which is often highly contextual. Virtually any transient lobby that promotes its interests directly, if not obscenely, can have a policy adopted.

A colleague once observed how intellectually incoherent cabinet meetings are in most developing countries. Under agenda item 1, the minister for transport might recommend deregulating taxis and privatising airlines. Agreed. Under item 2, the minister of finance recommends nationalising banks and instituting price controls. Agreed. No one queries the contradiction. In mature democracies, on the other hand, policies tend to be consistent with the established policy paradigm of the ruling party or coalition. In other words, influencing the climate of opinion in developing countries may be easier in the short term, because there are fewer people to influence and they are more easily influenced, but doing so is less enduring and less effective, because the climate of opinion is not a significant determinant of individual policies.

Second, individual policies in developing countries tend to be the consequence of a much less rigorous process of evaluation and debate than in developed countries. Typically, policies are initiated by self-serving vested interests. The process tends to be accompanied by seductive rhetoric. Finding a developed country with a similar policy to emulate is likely to be disproportionately effective. Checks and balances taken for granted in mature democracies, such as the separation of powers, are seldom included. A crude pseudo-intellectual policy document claims that the measure is 'international best practice'. Vested-interest lobbying is usually accompanied by support in cash and kind for whatever cause policymakers nominate – which may, of course, be themselves.

Mancur Olson's theory of collective action is particularly apt in developing countries – namely, that small vested interests seeking highly concentrated benefits at the expense of the widely dispersed general public are more effective than large vested interests seeking dispersed benefits, such as low-income consumers. Trench warfare in these circumstances entails mobilising countervailing interests, such as competitors, often at the proverbial eleventh hour. Where specialised vested interests are most effective (in developing countries), it 'cuts both ways', *against* and *for* classical liberals, who can, for instance, initiate rather than respond to policy development.

Sometimes trench warfare literally 'takes to the trenches', so to speak. In late November 2007, the Law Review Project worked on a high-profile march by residents of a historically black suburb, Alexandra, demanding restitution of land expropriated under apartheid. During the World Summit on Sustainable Development (WSSD, Johannesburg, 2002), we organised a 'freedom to trade' march on the Summit by hundreds of South African informal sector traders, Indian farmers and US students. Which is better, aerial bombardment or trench warfare? The answer is that the former is better *in the long run*. Which is preferable? That depends on context and priorities. When a country, such as contemporary Nepal, is in the process of drawing up a new constitution or considering major policy shifts, intensive trench warfare is effective. When, as in most mature democracies, there is relative political and economic stability, and policies tend to be a reflection of prevailing ideas, aerial bombardment is best. For countries in between, like South Africa, both are appropriate, shifting towards aerial bombardment as policies stabilise.

Relevance

Distinctions between aerial bombardment and trench warfare aside, an appreciation of which strategies and tactics in the war of ideas have been most effective historically is not necessarily instructive in the post-Cold-War world. Circumstances have changed so dramatically that previously effective strategies and tactics against ideologically explicit socialism, communism and fascism are unlikely to be effective henceforth. During the cold war, the war of ideas was clearly a clash of two readily identified titans, capitalism and socialism. The modern assault on liberty has different characteristics.

Liberty per se is no longer under explicit assault by people claiming that there are inherently superior alternatives (other than Islamists). The modern assault is more subtle and multifarious. Enemies of liberty do not define themselves as enemies; they often parade themselves as allies. Nobody of note propagates socialism, communism or fascism explicitly. People scarcely even propagate by name such once fashionable ideological concepts as 'the welfare state', 'social democracy' or 'the mixed economy'. That makes them harder to confront and protects them from being identified as enemies by the media and intellectuals. Protagonists of extreme regulation on a global scale see in climate change and terrorism opportunities for global feudalism. They are generally seen as benign and 'concerned', as wanting no more than to rescue 'the planet' from anthropogenic calamity – never as anti-liberty. They are latter-day Luddites in drag. That climate change *must* be harmful to man – whether or not it is – is a crucial ingredient, because it legitimises global control of every aspect of life, from pop concerts to deep-level mining, from sport to packaging, and from room temperature to transport.

Enemies of liberty not only seize upon fashionable catastrophism to legitimise dirigisme, but mangle truth in extraordinarily convoluted, often obscure and seductive ways. They get away with false or creative claims. They caricature anyone, however scientifically justified they may be, who questions the slightest aspect of their dogma as reactionary 'deniers'. Even people like me, who do not debate scientific orthodoxy, and query only *policy* recommendations, are presumed to be deniers. I have, for instance, been the victim of sustained media slander for supposedly being a climate change denier. Yet none of the elaborate attacks has cited a single source for my alleged denialism.

The war on liberty has all the ingredients of religious fanaticism, including excommunication of supposed heretics, and heresy is, as with all fanaticism, failure to agree with every detail. The difference between the current war of ideas and that which preceded it is that the 1970s equivalent of 'global warming', which was 'the population explosion', had to be positioned *within* the socialism–capitalism dichotomy. Now it is the other way round. Advocates of liberty have to position themselves within the climate change and war-on-terrorism discourses.

The observation that the new anti-liberty bogeys are 'climate change' (left) and the 'war on terrorism' (right) does not imply that concerns about either are not fully justified, only that they have been hijacked to serve the ends of the enemy in the war of ideas.

Many classical liberals, justifiably distressed by the extent to which real or exaggerated concerns are regarded as excuses for curtailing liberty, debate whether there really is serious climate change or terrorism – they are 'deniers'. Some argue instead that these threats are real but insignificant. Others insist that climate change is catastrophic, but that it is inevitable rather than man made, or that terrorism is a legitimate response to Western mischief, and that our responsibility is to 'understand them'. Another response is to produce elaborate theses to the effect that global warming is desirable, that it entails net benefits. And then there are those, like the International Policy Network (IPN), who argue compellingly that, regardless of the preceding debates, freedom and free markets are ideal policy responses. Those of us working for liberalisation in developing countries are particularly concerned about the implications for the world's poor billions of the world's rich millions using climate change to vindicate 'eco-imperialism'.

While classical liberals remain deeply divided on empirical aspects of climate change and terrorism, enemies of liberty march resolutely towards an ominous world where fantastic pro-freedom gains during recent decades may become a romantic memory for those of us old enough to recall the Cold War and the advent of the 21st century.

Regarding the war on terrorism, classical liberals of a more conservative disposition regard post-9/11 terrorism as a cataclysmic threat, which vindicates everything effective. Those who are more libertarian agonise about the implications for liberty. Their concern is that measures such as intercepting communications and anti-money-laundering rules are an unwarranted erosion of fundamental liberties. They are obviously right to be concerned. Their great challenge is to suggest effective alternatives consistent with classical liberal values.

There are other dimensions to the war of ideas, such as the perennial 'consumer protection' shibboleth. This is an area where classical liberal warriors are in serious need of reinforcements. Old myths are being recycled successfully in new guises in most countries. The world, in which doing everything has become easier, cheaper and safer, is misleadingly called 'the modern complex world', and that imaginary complexity is paraded as justifying intensified 'consumer protection'. What this rhetoric has in common is the assumption that there are 'free lunches' – that consumer benefits can be gained by counterproductive regulation at no direct or indirect cost to consumers – and that regulation affords better protection than free competition.

It may be that the emphasis on 'competition' plays into the hands of the enemy. Von Mises pointed out that in truly free markets people *collaborate* rather than *compete*. Entrepreneurial rivals do not so much 'out-compete' as 'out-cooperate' each other. Adam Smith's celebrated observation was that competitors seldom meet without resorting to *collaboration*. The sport analogy of free markets is unfortunate, because it suggests mistakenly that people interacting with each other in the economy have, as in athletics, a single winner, whereas all people transacting in markets are, with rare exceptions, winners.

In short, in these great war-of-ideas battlefields, classical liberals face completely new challenges. We are still confined to operating within one or both of two broad strategies, *intellectual* aerial bombardment and *tactical* trench warfare, but cannot do so by simply recycling what served us well before. There is no longer a crude binary clash of ideas. It was easy and sometimes obvious to decide what to do when capitalism/liberalism fought communism/socialism. But now the arguments against freedom and markets are more obtuse and surreptitious. They tend to be from people who *say* they are for markets. To be relevant, classical liberalism now has to be advanced less as a fight of good against evil and more in terms of bona fide differences between kindred spirits in mutual pursuit of the good society.

There are many manifestations of this new foggy world of ideas, the most obvious being that the clear paradigm difference between political parties has all but vanished. The position the British Conservative, Labour and Liberal Democrat parties, the American Democrats and Republicans, or the German CDU and SDP are likely to adopt on a given issue is no longer as predictable as it was before the 1990s. There are no more clear fault lines distinguishing them.

Projects

One of the most effective projects in which the IEA and the Free Market Foundation (FMF) are involved is the production, with Canada's Fraser Institute playing the leading role, of the Economic Freedom of the World index. This, together with the Heritage Foundation–*Wall Street Journal* Economic Freedom Index (EFI) and Freedom House's Freedom Index, has enabled activists and decision-makers to identify the individual components in the complex policy mix of individual countries that enhance the likelihood of achieving policy objectives. Having noted the power of these indices to influence policymakers, we decided that the current world context needs something less overtly ideological which correlates a wide range of specific policy objectives (as opposed to such generic objectives as economic growth) more directly with individual policies (as opposed to baskets of policies). Accordingly, we took a pioneering step towards a fundamentally new approach, which we published as *Habits of Highly Effective Countries: Lessons for South Africa* (*Habits*), in the hope that in due course versions will be produced for other countries.

Habits builds on the positive experience of economic freedom indices but is fundamentally different in important respects. First, it is not informed by any philosophical concepts such as 'economic freedom', 'competitiveness' (World Economic Forum), 'freedom' (Freedom House), and so on. It is essentially an exercise in statistics. It asks what we call 'a policymakers' question', which is: 'Which policies in the world's experience coincide with success and failure at achieving individual policy objectives?'

Our thinking is that in a world in which there are no longer distinctive policy paradigms it will become increasingly important for classical liberals to fight the war of ideas in ways that appear overtly to be 'neutral'. This means that we will identify and publicise that which works in practice more than that which is morally or philosophically consistent with liberty. It is unfortunate for us to have to make this shift. We are more comfortable with and experienced at the defence of the principles of liberty. It is extremely hard work to identify and calculate empirical links between policy variables and outcomes. They are subject to sophisticated and complex debate and critique. Most importantly, it is very difficult to 'translate' complex statistical variables and correlations into language and forms that are readily understood by lay people. This, however, is what we regard as our challenge for the coming decades.

In *Habits*, now also available as a DVD video, we identify the policy characteristics of 'winners' and 'losers' with reference to all the major policy objectives of government. Which policies, for instance, coincide with higher or lower rates of crime, literacy, housing, health, sanitation, GDP or capital formation? By converting our message from being overtly ideological to being empirical, we believe that we will enhance our relevance as we move into the new circumstances of the 21st century.

Conclusion

The war of ideas must continue to be fought by aerial bombardment and trench warfare but, like all modern warfare, has to deploy new strategies and tactics. Research and publications, for instance, should embrace modern technology (concise and free to download). We have to confront new threats to liberty which are less obvious or readily classifiable than communism, socialism or fascism. We still need the right people doing the right thing at the right time in the right place, doing their best to understand what determines the course of events in the great spontaneous Hayekian order of ideas.

14 HOW THE ASSOCIATION FOR LIBERAL THINKING IS CHANGING THE CLIMATE OF OPINION IN TURKEY

Atilla Yayla, Association for Liberal Thinking (Turkey)

Turkey does not have a strong cultural tradition of respecting individual rights, private property and free enterprise. Despite exaggerated claims that the country made a completely new start in 1923, when the Turkish republic was founded, little, if anything, changed, either culturally or in the way public authority was structured and used in social, economic, cultural and political life. The Ottoman Empire did not provide Turkey with full official and legal recognition of private property because it feared that strengthening private property holders and independent entrepreneurs could threaten the authority of the state. In addition, civil society institutions had not been aware of the need to limit the use of political authority. There were some developments in that direction during the last years of the empire, but they were interrupted by World War I and the empire disintegrated at the end of the war. When the new republic was founded, its leaders aimed to modernise and Westernise the country. This did not translate, however, into the new ruling elite establishing the rule of law, a free market economy, separation of powers, or a limited and constitutional government. The new ruling elite, in fact, attempted a social engineering project to reshape society. This is revealed by the words of the Tenth Year Anthem: 'we created fifteen million youngsters at any age in ten years of the Republic'.

By the 1980s almost every intellectual believed in right or left versions of collectivism. Few believed in private property and the market economy. In the economics departments of Turkish universities, various types of collectivism and anti-market tendencies dominated the climate of opinion. The mildest form of anti-capitalist thought that existed was perhaps Keynesianism. Intellectuals believed in a strong state that would dominate society, take care of every citizen, create wealth and exercise social justice. It was almost impossible to find an article or book that defended private property, the free market economy, competition or free enterprise. The alternative was not to be a free marketeer; rather, it was fashionable to be a right-wing collectivist against left-wing collectivists or vice versa.

In the years that followed, this was bound to change. The story of the Association for Liberal Thinking (ALT) started with two young academics: Mustafa Erdogan and me. I had graduated from the Department of Economics in the Faculty of Politics at Ankara University and could be described as a right-wing socialist. Mustafa Erdogan graduated from the Law Faculty of the same university. We met in the late 1970s and by the early 1980s we had become close friends. As right-wing socialists we were unhappy, both with our ideological positions and the situation in our country. After months of debates and observations of our age group and country, we came to feel isolated and alienated from intellectual circles. We rejected the beliefs commonly held by other young people. These feelings were compounded by the fact that we exhibited a natural loathing for authority – especially arbitrary authority. We loved freedom, and this was what saved us from becoming true believers in anti-freedom. To get rid of our feelings of loneliness and to produce civilised solutions to problems created by this situation, we started reading day and night. Every day we learned something new about freedom, and we started to share these ideas with one another. This continued for several years. As the 1980s came to a close, we discovered what we believed in: individual freedom, private property, the free market economy, individual initiative and the minimal state. We then knew that we were classical liberals or libertarians.

While we were fortunate not to be alone in a country of 60 million, there were only two of us, and that was not enough. We were like a drop in the ocean, and it was crucial to change this situation. We spent the late 1980s thinking about what to do and decided to initiate an opinion movement. Eventually we got in touch with Professor Norman Barry of Buckingham University and paid him a visit in the summer of 1992. While in London, I visited the Institute of Economic Affairs and was given a scholarship to participate in the 1992 Mont Pèlerin Society General Meeting in Vancouver, Canada. At that meeting, I met numerous defenders of the free market, including Milton Friedman and James Buchanan. This meeting was encouraging because I learned that our loneliness was limited to Turkey, not the rest of the world. We were inspired to go forward with our plan to defend and disseminate free market ideas under the roof of an organisation.

Our group expanded by 50 per cent when Kazim Berzeg, a lawyer and long-time libertarian, discovered and joined us in the autumn of 1992. On 26 December 1992, we inaugurated our intellectual movement: the Association for Liberal Thinking. In the beginning, we had no office, no facilities and no legal status. Furthermore, at that time, it was dangerous even to use the label liberal. We had regular meetings for more than a year in a restaurant called Pigalle in the centre of Ankara. Then Kazim Berzeg offered to let us use a dark and unoccupied room in his office near Pigalle as the ALT's base. He also allowed the ALT to use his phone, fax and typing machines. Shortly after this, I invited two of my talented students, Gozde Ergozen and Ozlem Caglar, to work part time for the Association. Thus the ALT had an office and communication facilities and a few months later, on 1 April 1994, it was registered and received its official status. Today, the ALT occupies two full apartments in the city centre and has four full-time staff and many volunteers.

Over the years, ALT developed, step by step, into an institution. It started its publishing history with a little quarterly leaflet containing a few articles, book reviews and news items. In 1995, with a grant from the Atlas Economic Research Foundation (United States), we published our first book: F. A. Hayek's *The Road to Serfdom.* This was followed by numerous other books, and now our publications number almost two hundred. Liberte is the imprint for ALT's publications and they are distributed in bookshops and online at www.liberte.com.tr. ALT started its quarterly journal, *Liberal Thought,* in 1996, and over time it has become a prestigious academic journal. In 2002, we started a second quarterly economic journal, *Piyasa (Market),* but it was discontinued in 2005 to avoid splitting our readership. ALT was among the first NGOs in Turkey to have a website, and this features free market articles. We concentrated our efforts to strengthen the liberal position on electronic publishing and now publish daily commentaries from the free market perspective in a separate electronic journal, www.hurfikirler.com (free ideas).

To promote a tradition of classical liberal/libertarian thinking, books were indispensable to us. We had to work like an academy when training people in the ideas of liberty, because it was almost impossible for a person to hear and learn about these ideas in the faculties of Turkish universities. Since 1995 we have developed lectures on concepts such as the rule of law, individual rights, free market economics, liberal democracy and classical liberal/ libertarian philosophy. In the beginning we organised speeches every Friday evening and subsequently we have developed a series of seminars on these topics for a variety of NGOs, youth groups and political parties, which we hold in Ankara as well as other cities throughout the country. Currently, we hold regular weekend seminars under the 'Liberty School' title at our premises. These seminars are also held in numerous cities across Turkey so that they can include regional participants active in universities, NGOs, bar associations, trade chambers, business associations and local radio or television channels. Over three thousand people have now graduated from 'Liberty School'.

Another aspect of our early activities included holding debates in different cities all over Turkey. We organised panel discussions in more than thirty cities on 'Political and Economical Liberalism', 'Islam, Civil Society and the Free Market Economy', 'Freedom of Expression' and 'Liberal Democracy'. These debates were either theoretical or addressed contemporary Turkish problems. The participation of local groups encouraged free-market organisa- tions to expand and become centres of intellectual activism in their own area. Sometimes the local debates were enriched with weekend seminars, local TV appearances or workshops with local opinion leaders.

Apart from panel discussions, the ALT has organised almost twenty national and international symposia which served as important gatherings for interested partners. These have helped expose intellectuals, public policy experts, bureaucrats, decision-makers, politicians, lawmakers and journalists to free market ideas.

The ALT, with its strategy of encouraging a classical liberal/ libertarian intellectual tradition, has helped to cultivate many young academics and thinkers. Our senior founders helped junior intellectuals in their studies and encouraged them to join academia. Today there are numerous senior classical liberal or libertarian academics and experts who can contribute to our mission. We now run an academic advisory service to help strengthen academic talents. We maintain a network of classical liberal intellectuals throughout Turkey and hold an annual 'Congress' to bring together academics, lawyers, journalists, bureaucrats, politicians, authors, free-market-oriented groups and promising young students to discuss liberal ideas. In these meetings the participants have the opportunity to meet other like-minded people and to explore areas of collaboration. People coming from all different parts of the country can feel that they are not alone in their thinking, as we were in the beginning. In addition to our annual Congress, each year the ALT holds a Freedom Dinner to bring together the defenders of liberty from all over Turkey and to reward a freedom fighter with a Freedom Award.

We have also established autonomous research centres to support independent studies and market-friendly solutions. They include centres for the study of educational policy, environmental issues, religion and liberty, and economic freedom.

From 2001 to 2003 the ALT conducted the biggest civil society project ever undertaken in Turkey. The project was on freedom of expression and was sponsored by the European Commission. It was very important for the ALT to contribute to this vital issue in

Turkey, in terms of providing the theoretical principles required to strengthen legal protection. The project was very timely because at that time Turkey was in the process of meeting the Copenhagen criteria of the European Union and was engaged in some related legal reforms. The debates and the literature offered by the ALT were an important influence on the judges, public prosecutors, academics and intellectuals.

The ALT also completed a one-year project on religious freedom – another vital issue – in 2005. We brought together representatives of different Muslim and non-Muslim communities, as well as researchers and academics, to discuss relevant problems, and developed solutions based on the principles of individual rights, religious freedom, freedom of association, the rule of law and limited government. As a result of the remarkable success of this programme, the ALT was awarded the Freda Utley Prize for Advancing Liberty from the Atlas Economic Research Foundation. The ALT is also very proud to have received the Templeton Institute of Excellence Award from Atlas in 2004.

The ALT has developed many international partners within the Atlas network. Through these international fellowships we receive many opportunities to collaborate with others to further develop our capacity and enhance our influence in Turkey.

Over time the activities of the ALT have expanded and gained stability. Today we concentrate on educational efforts, publishing and advising. When Professor Erdogan, Mr Berzeg and I started this intellectual movement, we never dreamed that the ALT would be so successful and influential. We have been sincere in our struggle and have desired freedom and prosperity, not only for ourselves, but for all our fellow citizens and all of humanity. Without a doubt, the strong ideas that we promote have been like a lighthouse for everyone and every group in Turkey. The classical liberal arguments we have offered have been utilised to legitimise the struggle of every individual or group whose rights have been violated. In the past fifteen years, we have advised various political parties, recommended free market economic policies to politicians and strived to improve freedom.

Throughout all this, we believed in the power of ideas. In our efforts we tried to combine professionalism with idealism. We did not seek positions in politics or bureaucracy and did not try to transform the ALT into a political movement. Instead we wanted to develop a strong movement of classical liberal/libertarian intellectuals.

While following this strategy we paid special attention to making sure that we maintained a constructive approach towards newcomers and were consistent in being comprehensive, pluralist, respectful and honest. We did not want to remain on the margins; rather, we worked hard to become an influential and 'dominant' intellectual group. We had to be a focal point for academics, media professionals, business people, university students and all other intellectuals. Since individualist thinking was so rare in Turkey, we needed to create a freedom movement to infiltrate into not only political studies and economics, but also history, literature and the arts.

We realise that we do not need to be the practitioners; as the transmitters of the ideas, however, we have to influence the politicians, bureaucrats and intellectuals. To maintain the autonomy and credibility of the ALT, we also remain alert to financial or political entanglements that could undermine our efforts.

Today the ALT has become the nation's most important intellectual movement. Without hesitation we can claim that, one day, those individuals who were brought up with the ideas that the ALT defends will run Turkey. After just fifteen years we can already see the fruits of the seeds that we have spread around the country.

ABOUT THE IEA

The Institute is a research and educational charity (No. CC 235 351), limited by guarantee. Its mission is to improve understanding of the fundamental institutions of a free society by analysing and expounding the role of markets in solving economic and social problems.

The IEA achieves its mission by:

- a high-quality publishing programme
- conferences, seminars, lectures and other events
- outreach to school and college students
- brokering media introductions and appearances

The IEA, which was established in 1955 by the late Sir Antony Fisher, is an educational charity, not a political organisation. It is independent of any political party or group and does not carry on activities intended to affect support for any political party or candidate in any election or referendum, or at any other time. It is financed by sales of publications, conference fees and voluntary donations.

In addition to its main series of publications the IEA also publishes a quarterly journal, *Economic Affairs*.

The IEA is aided in its work by a distinguished international Academic Advisory Council and an eminent panel of Honorary Fellows. Together with other academics, they review prospective IEA publications, their comments being passed on anonymously to authors. All IEA papers are therefore subject to the same rigorous independent refereeing process as used by leading academic journals.

IEA publications enjoy widespread classroom use and course adoptions in schools and universities. They are also sold throughout the world and often translated/reprinted.

Since 1974 the IEA has helped to create a worldwide network of 100 similar institutions in over 70 countries. They are all independent but share the IEA's mission.

Views expressed in the IEA's publications are those of the authors, not those of the Institute (which has no corporate view), its Managing Trustees, Academic Advisory Council members or senior staff.

Members of the Institute's Academic Advisory Council, Honorary Fellows, Trustees and Staff are listed on the following page.

The Institute gratefully acknowledges financial support for its publications programme and other work from a generous benefaction by the late Alec and Beryl Warren.

The Institute of Economic Affairs
2 Lord North Street, Westminster, London SW1P 3LB
Tel: 020 7799 8900
Fax: 020 7799 2137
Email: iea@iea.org.uk
Internet: iea.org.uk

Other papers recently published by the IEA include:

WHO, What and Why?
Transnational Government, Legitimacy and the World Health Organization
Roger Scruton
Occasional Paper 113; ISBN 0 255 36487 3; £8.00

The World Turned Rightside Up
A New Trading Agenda for the Age of Globalisation
John C. Hulsman
Occasional Paper 114; ISBN 0 255 36495 4; £8.00

The Representation of Business in English Literature
Introduced and edited by Arthur Pollard
Readings 53; ISBN 0 255 36491 1; £12.00

Anti-Liberalism 2000
The Rise of New Millennium Collectivism
David Henderson
Occasional Paper 115; ISBN 0 255 36497 0; £7.50

Capitalism, Morality and Markets
Brian Griffiths, Robert A. Sirico, Norman Barry & Frank Field
Readings 54; ISBN 0 255 36496 2; £7.50

A Conversation with Harris and Seldon
Ralph Harris & Arthur Seldon
Occasional Paper 116; ISBN 0 255 36498 9; £7.50

Malaria and the DDT Story
Richard Tren & Roger Bate
Occasional Paper 117; ISBN 0 255 36499 7; £10.00

A Plea to Economists Who Favour Liberty: Assist the Everyman
Daniel B. Klein
Occasional Paper 118; ISBN 0 255 36501 2; £10.00

The Changing Fortunes of Economic Liberalism

Yesterday, Today and Tomorrow
David Henderson
Occasional Paper 105 (new edition); ISBN 0 255 36520 9; £12.50

The Global Education Industry

Lessons from Private Education in Developing Countries
James Tooley
Hobart Paper 141 (new edition); ISBN 0 255 36503 9; £12.50

Saving Our Streams

The Role of the Anglers' Conservation Association in
Protecting English and Welsh Rivers
Roger Bate
Research Monograph 53; ISBN 0 255 36494 6; £10.00

Better Off Out?

The Benefits or Costs of EU Membership
Brian Hindley & Martin Howe
Occasional Paper 99 (new edition); ISBN 0 255 36502 0; £10.00

Buckingham at 25

Freeing the Universities from State Control
Edited by James Tooley
Readings 55; ISBN 0 255 36512 8; £15.00

Lectures on Regulatory and Competition Policy

Irwin M. Stelzer
Occasional Paper 120; ISBN 0 255 36511 x; £12.50

Misguided Virtue

False Notions of Corporate Social Responsibility
David Henderson
Hobart Paper 142; ISBN 0 255 36510 1; £12.50

HIV and Aids in Schools
The Political Economy of Pressure Groups and Miseducation
Barrie Craven, Pauline Dixon, Gordon Stewart & James Tooley
Occasional Paper 121; ISBN 0 255 36522 5; £10.00

The Road to Serfdom
The Reader's Digest *condensed version*
Friedrich A. Hayek
Occasional Paper 122; ISBN 0 255 36530 6; £7.50

Bastiat's *The Law*
Introduction by Norman Barry
Occasional Paper 123; ISBN 0 255 36509 8; £7.50

A Globalist Manifesto for Public Policy
Charles Calomiris
Occasional Paper 124; ISBN 0 255 36525 x; £7.50

Euthanasia for Death Duties
Putting Inheritance Tax Out of Its Misery
Barry Bracewell-Milnes
Research Monograph 54; ISBN 0 255 36513 6; £10.00

Liberating the Land
The Case for Private Land-use Planning
Mark Pennington
Hobart Paper 143; ISBN 0 255 36508 x; £10.00

IEA Yearbook of Government Performance 2002/2003
Edited by Peter Warburton
Yearbook 1; ISBN 0 255 36532 2; £15.00

Britain's Relative Economic Performance, 1870–1999
Nicholas Crafts
Research Monograph 55; ISBN 0 255 36524 1; £10.00

Should We Have Faith in Central Banks?
Otmar Issing
Occasional Paper 125; ISBN 0 255 36528 4; £7.50

The Dilemma of Democracy
Arthur Seldon
Hobart Paper 136 (reissue); ISBN 0 255 36536 5; £10.00

Capital Controls: a 'Cure' Worse Than the Problem?
Forrest Capie
Research Monograph 56; ISBN 0 255 36506 3; £10.00

The Poverty of 'Development Economics'
Deepak Lal
Hobart Paper 144 (reissue); ISBN 0 255 36519 5; £15.00

Should Britain Join the Euro?
The Chancellor's Five Tests Examined
Patrick Minford
Occasional Paper 126; ISBN 0 255 36527 6; £7.50

Post-Communist Transition: Some Lessons
Leszek Balcerowicz
Occasional Paper 127; ISBN 0 255 36533 0; £7.50

A Tribute to Peter Bauer
John Blundell et al.
Occasional Paper 128; ISBN 0 255 36531 4; £10.00

Employment Tribunals
Their Growth and the Case for Radical Reform
J. R. Shackleton
Hobart Paper 145; ISBN 0 255 36515 2; £10.00

Fifty Economic Fallacies Exposed
Geoffrey E. Wood
Occasional Paper 129; ISBN 0 255 36518 7; £12.50

Economy and Virtue
Essays on the Theme of Markets and Morality
Edited by Dennis O'Keeffe
Readings 59; ISBN 0 255 36504 7; £12.50

Free Markets Under Siege
Cartels, Politics and Social Welfare
Richard A. Epstein
Occasional Paper 132; ISBN 0 255 36553 5; £10.00

Unshackling Accountants
D. R. Myddelton
Hobart Paper 149; ISBN 0 255 36559 4; £12.50

The Euro as Politics
Pedro Schwartz
Research Monograph 58; ISBN 0 255 36535 7; £12.50

Pricing Our Roads
Vision and Reality
Stephen Glaister & Daniel J. Graham
Research Monograph 59; ISBN 0 255 36562 4; £10.00

The Role of Business in the Modern World
Progress, Pressures, and Prospects for the Market Economy
David Henderson
Hobart Paper 150; ISBN 0 255 36548 9; £12.50

Public Service Broadcasting Without the BBC?
Alan Peacock
Occasional Paper 133; ISBN 0 255 36565 9; £10.00

The ECB and the Euro: the First Five Years
Otmar Issing
Occasional Paper 134; ISBN 0 255 36555 1; £10.00

Towards a Liberal Utopia?
Edited by Philip Booth
Hobart Paperback 32; ISBN 0 255 36563 2; £15.00

The Way Out of the Pensions Quagmire
Philip Booth & Deborah Cooper
Research Monograph 60; ISBN 0 255 36517 9; £12.50

Black Wednesday
A Re-examination of Britain's Experience in the Exchange Rate Mechanism
Alan Budd
Occasional Paper 135; ISBN 0 255 36566 7; £7.50

Crime: Economic Incentives and Social Networks
Paul Ormerod
Hobart Paper 151; ISBN 0 255 36554 3; £10.00

The Road to Serfdom *with* **The Intellectuals and Socialism**
Friedrich A. Hayek
Occasional Paper 136; ISBN 0 255 36576 4; £10.00

Money and Asset Prices in Boom and Bust
Tim Congdon
Hobart Paper 152; ISBN 0 255 36570 5; £10.00

The Dangers of Bus Re-regulation
and Other Perspectives on Markets in Transport
John Hibbs et al.
Occasional Paper 137; ISBN 0 255 36572 1; £10.00

The New Rural Economy
Change, Dynamism and Government Policy
Berkeley Hill et al.
Occasional Paper 138; ISBN 0 255 36546 2; £15.00

The Benefits of Tax Competition
Richard Teather
Hobart Paper 153; ISBN 0 255 36569 1; £12.50

Wheels of Fortune
Self-funding Infrastructure and the Free Market Case for a Land Tax
Fred Harrison
Hobart Paper 154; ISBN 0 255 36589 6; £12.50

Were 364 Economists All Wrong?
Edited by Philip Booth
Readings 60; ISBN 978 0 255 36588 8; £10.00

Europe After the 'No' Votes
Mapping a New Economic Path
Patrick A. Messerlin
Occasional Paper 139; ISBN 978 0 255 36580 2; £10.00

The Railways, the Market and the Government
John Hibbs et al.
Readings 61; ISBN 978 0 255 36567 3; £12.50

Corruption: The World's Big C
Cases, Causes, Consequences, Cures
Ian Senior
Research Monograph 61; ISBN 978 0 255 36571 0; £12.50

Choice and the End of Social Housing
Peter King
Hobart Paper 155; ISBN 978 0 255 36568 0; £10.00

Sir Humphrey's Legacy
Facing Up to the Cost of Public Sector Pensions
Neil Record
Hobart Paper 156; ISBN 978 0 255 36578 9; £10.00

The Economics of Law
Cento Veljanovski
Second edition
Hobart Paper 157; ISBN 978 0 255 36561 1; £12.50

Living with Leviathan
Public Spending, Taxes and Economic Performance
David B. Smith
Hobart Paper 158; ISBN 978 0 255 36579 6; £12.50

The Vote Motive
Gordon Tullock
New edition
Hobart Paperback 33; ISBN 978 0 255 36577 2; £10.00

Waging the War of Ideas
John Blundell
Third edition
Occasional Paper 131; ISBN 978 0 255 36606 9; £12.50

The War Between the State and the Family
How Government Divides and Impoverishes
Patricia Morgan
Hobart Paper 159; ISBN 978 0 255 36596 3; £10.00

Capitalism – A Condensed Version
Arthur Seldon
Occasional Paper 140; ISBN 978 0 255 36598 7; £7.50

Catholic Social Teaching and the Market Economy
Edited by Philip Booth
Hobart Paperback 34; ISBN 978 0 255 36581 9; £15.00

Adam Smith – A Primer
Eamonn Butler
Occasional Paper 141; ISBN 978 0 255 36608 3; £7.50

Happiness, Economics and Public Policy
Helen Johns & Paul Ormerod
Research Monograph 62; ISBN 978 0 255 36600 7; £10.00

They Meant Well
Government Project Disasters
D. R. Myddelton
Hobart Paper 160; ISBN 978 0 255 36601 4; £12.50

Rescuing Social Capital from Social Democracy
John Meadowcroft & Mark Pennington
Hobart Paper 161; ISBN 978 0 255 36592 5; £10.00

Paths to Property
Approaches to Institutional Change in International Development
Karol Boudreaux & Paul Dragos Aligica
Hobart Paper 162; ISBN 978 0 255 36582 6; £10.00

Prohibitions
Edited by John Meadowcroft
Hobart Paperback 35; ISBN 978 0 255 36585 7; £15.00

Trade Policy, New Century
The WTO, FTAs and Asia Rising
Razeen Sally
Hobart Paper 163; ISBN 978 0 255 36544 4; £12.50

Sixty Years On – Who Cares for the NHS?
Helen Evans
Research Monograph 63; ISBN 978 0 255 36611 3; £10.00

Other IEA publications

Comprehensive information on other publications and the wider work of the IEA can be found at www.iea.org.uk. To order any publication please see below.

Personal customers

Orders from personal customers should be directed to the IEA:
Bob Layson
IEA
2 Lord North Street
FREEPOST LON10168
London SW1P 3YZ
Tel: 020 7799 8909. Fax: 020 7799 2137
Email: blayson@iea.org.uk

Trade customers

All orders from the book trade should be directed to the IEA's distributor:
Gazelle Book Services Ltd (IEA Orders)
FREEPOST RLYS-EAHU-YSCZ
White Cross Mills
Hightown
Lancaster LA1 4XS
Tel: 01524 68765, Fax: 01524 53232
Email: sales@gazellebooks.co.uk

IEA subscriptions

The IEA also offers a subscription service to its publications. For a single annual payment (currently £42.00 in the UK), subscribers receive every monograph the IEA publishes. For more information please contact:
Adam Myers
Subscriptions
IEA
2 Lord North Street
FREEPOST LON10168
London SW1P 3YZ
Tel: 020 7799 8920, Fax: 020 7799 2137
Email: amyers@iea.org.uk